# The *Art*
# of *Auditioning*

**A Handbook for Singers,
Accompanists and Coaches**
by Anthony Legge

London • Frankfurt am Main • Leipzig • New York

**Peters Edition Limited**
10–12 Baches Street
London
N1 6DN

Tel: 020 7553 4000
Fax: 020 7490 4921
email: sales@uk.edition-peters.com
internet: www.edition-peters.com

First published 2001
© 2001 by Hinrichsen Edition, Peters Edition Limited, London

ISBN 1 901507 56 4

A catalogue record for this book is
available from the British Library

Photo: AKG London / Jost Schilgen
Book design by adamhaydesign.com
Typset in Adobe Garamond
Music engraving by Figaro
Printed by Caligraving Limited, Thetford, Norfolk, England

# Contents

# Preface

When the idea of writing this book first came to me, I felt there was a 'vacuum of knowledge' among singers about the technique of auditioning. Since the book has come into print, the reaction to it has demonstrated to me how deep that need was, and how important it is to help singers present themselves in the best possible way.

A brilliant painting still needs a good, suitable frame to bring out all its facets, and painters are aware of the vital effect that the right frame brings to each work that they execute. So, in the same way, singers should be encouraged to 'sell their talents' and to discover just how well the ideas and feelings that they are trying to communicate really do get over the footlights. If this book can help in even a small way, I will be very honoured.

I am aware that the position of some of the arias within the different *Fächer* are, to some degree, controversial. Ideally, roles should not be compartmentalized in any way, but for many opera companies and agents some system needs to be adopted to aid them in their difficult task of casting so many different roles. I hope that some of the suggested placings of these roles will stimulate the reader's own perception of the vocal and musical strengths and weaknesses demonstrated by each aria. I also hope that accompanists will find the book useful for learning the repertoire and helping singers to choose new material for learning, even if they decide ultimately not to use a particular aria for audition purposes.

I would like to thank once more my many colleagues who have, over many years, given me much encouragement and the benefit of their knowledge. I am grateful to Linda Hawken for inspiring me to prepare this new Peters edition, mindful that the company has issued so many useful publications of much of the repertoire mentioned in this book.

*Anthony Legge*

# Introduction

Auditioning is an experience that you, as a singer, cannot avoid. You may find yourself singing for a panel of judges at a competition or festival, for an agent, for the representatives of a music society or orchestra, or for an opera company. An audition is the simplest and, until someone discovers a better alternative, the best way for you to show off your qualities to those people who may wish to employ or reward you.

Since you cannot avoid auditioning – and very few singers enjoy their brief moments on the audition platform – it seems sensible to try and face up to the whole problem from the start. This book is designed to help you to find a simple and effective way to present your capabilities and talents to greatest advantage.

One way for competition and festival judges, agents, administrators, producers and conductors to discover the qualities of singers is to hear them in performance but, unfortunately, this is not always possible. It is important to put yourself in the shoes of those who are going to listen to you: they want you to sing at your best because they are looking for the most thrilling and exciting talent they can find, and when they find it they will be quite delighted.

Luck plays a significant part in a singer's career. You need to be offering an audition panel precisely the qualities they are looking for at a given time. The singer may be compared to a very special coat displayed in a shop window. Passers-by may stop and admire it but, because of the hot weather, decide that it is not what they are looking for there and then. The reason for which a singer is not chosen may be very different from the one that he or she imagines.

Those singers who wish to make a career outside the world of opera will generally find themselves auditioning for specific repertoire or engagements. They will often know which piece of music is to be performed and can thus prepare an appropriate audition aria or song. Lists of songs, oratorios, etc. may be found in many books, especially American editions such as *Singers Repertoire* by Berton Coffin (Scarecrow Press, New York 1960) or *Music for the Voice* by Sergius Kagen (Indiana University Press 1968).

When auditioning for an opera company, it can sometimes happen that a singer knows for which opera he or she is being auditioned but, in general, one finds that a company or agent is looking for a voice type rather than someone to fill a specific role. The system of voice types is most utilized in German-speaking opera houses, and the German *Fach* system is explained on pages 44–9. Opera singers need to be fully aware of the demands of an entire role when offering an aria to an audition panel. For this reason, I have compiled in Part II a selection of operatic repertoire, set out in accordance with the *Fach* system (see my comment on this in the Preface), specifically high-lighting the difficulties and advantages of each aria, together with my reasons for choosing it. Part III provides the singer with a life-long reference list of arias suitable for operatic auditions, including many additional pieces, for instance, some Handel arias. This information will also be of great value to accompanists, giving them a clear guide as to what to expect when playing for auditions.

# Part I
# Audition
# Technique

# The right approach

One of the most fundamental decisions for you to make is to establish exactly what kind of singer you are and in what field you have most to offer. Be realistic and yet do not undersell yourself. Whatever you choose to sing must be fully within your capabilities, both vocally and emotionally, and must be music you could perform 'standing on your head'.

Singing is about one simple concept – *communication.* The audition panel is only interested in what 'comes across the footlights'. You may find that some singers are not as vocally or musically proficient as you, but they may have a great ability to communicate. The panel is looking to see what you communicate when you first walk into the audition room or on to the stage – assuredness, generosity of character, and a philosophical attitude to the outcome of the audition. When you first start to sing the panel immediately recognizes, in the same way that the public can, the quality and timbre of your voice and, if you have chosen a suitable aria, can also recognize your vocal and dynamic range. If it is a well-experienced panel, the members need less time to make their judgements, so a long aria is not always expedient, especially when the panel has so many other singers to hear. It is very hard to face these truths in their raw state, for the singing profession is not an easy one; often the hard facts about your singing ability will be said behind your back. If you are going to be a successful singer, nothing will put you off. The panel knows that if you can audition successfully, there is a good chance that you can perform successfully: the latter is so much easier in comparison. Of course there are exceptions to the rule, and there have been cases where good auditions have not led to good performances, but this is not your problem. Your concern is to present the best possible package to those darkly lit people in the stalls.

Surprisingly enough, the panel is often slightly nervous of your attitude towards them. Why is this? There have been occasions when a highly strung singer has misunderstood the panel's necessarily detached approach as being a lack of interest, and has reacted badly. If a panel has had such an experience, its members may be rather wary, so do not be put off by this. It is best to help the panel to feel at ease while at the same time letting them feel that something special is about to happen. In other words, treat an audition as you would a true performance to a paying audience.

### What music should you choose?

Festivals and competitions usually publish a list of set works to be prepared with the possible inclusion of a few 'own choice' arias. Obviously you will choose the music that you can sing best, that you like, and that shows off all your qualities. You should select contrasting items and not find yourself singing just fast, brilliant music or, on the other hand, only music which is slow and languourous. Try to get a good combination of pieces, as you would if preparing a well-balanced menu. For oratorio auditions you will need to demonstrate your range of styles – Bach, Haydn, Brahms and Tippett, for instance. In most cases you should sing your choice in the original language, unless the festival or competition specifies that it is to be sung in translation. For opera companies that perform in the vernacular, you need to find a good translation, or an aria written in the appropriate language.

The number of arias you will need to present may depend on the requirements of the audition panel, but a common and ideal compromise is for the singer to select the first aria (your 'war-horse') and to let the panel choose a second one from a small selection. If they are short arias, the panel may even want to hear a third. Of course, if your war-horse is moderately long, with a variety of emotions and styles of music (for example, recitative, cavatina, cabaletta), only the one aria may be needed. So be prepared! But the most important requirement is that these arias should be *contrasting*. This word is hard to define but, in very naïve terms, it means fast and slow: in other words, one with character, declamation, coloratura or a combination of all of these, and the other to show off legato singing, control of slow or soft singing, and bel canto (as opposed to soubrette).

Most panels prefer repertoire arias, even though they may have heard them a thousand times. These arias demonstrate what they want to discover about your voice and are generally well composed. If you choose an unusual aria, it must demonstrate something very special, or be a truly exhilarating war-horse, brilliant and concise. The panel is not interested in being shown how cleverly you attack a musically difficult aria – it is looking for opera singers! An example of a dangerous choice is Baba the Turk's aria from Stravinsky's *The Rake's Progress*. It is hard both for singer and pianist, and only demonstrates wide leaps, diction, and one emotion, that of angry nagging – not beauty of voice, line, changes of colour and dramatic skill. It gives no hint of what else you could sing.

When you audition for a salaried principal job in an opera house, the panel will be looking to see which roles will suit your voice, stature and ability, and how they could best utilize you within their present company. This is especially true in Germany where they will be deciding on which *Fach* you belong to, and the roles you could sing during your contractual term.

In Germany, *Fach* is a very special term, giving a standard description of your voice and thus defining which roles you will sing. The operas will already have been planned for the year and the panel will need to fill the gaps in the cast lists, utilizing your voice to its fullest extent. These standard descriptions of voice types and the roles associated with them can be found in *Handbuch der Oper* by R. Kloiber (published by Bärenreiter in two volumes).

Some of the choices of roles associated with certain voice types can be quite surprising: for example, Marzelline (*Fidelio*) as Soubrette or Lyric Coloratura Soprano, Musetta (*La bohème*) also as Soubrette or Lyric Coloratura Soprano, Cherubino (*Le nozze di Figaro*) as Lyric Soprano. Many other instances may be noticed. (In Part II of this book there is a list of arias and descriptions of these voice types.) In Germany, since opera is so much more a business than a vocation, the audition panel tends to assume that, if you present an aria, you can sing the entire role. Frequently, however, the arias are not the most difficult parts of a role. For instance, the two arias of Azucena from *Il trovatore* – 'Stride la vampa' and 'Condotta ell'era in ceppi' – do not show that you can sing the Manrico/Azucena duet or the Azucena interrogation in Conte di Luna's war-camp.

Wherever you audition, it is above all necessary to understand the way in which the agents, administrators, and so on, are thinking. As with all the singers that pass through the audition room, they are bound to put you in a mental box with a label, simply as a method of remembering you. It is therefore important that you try to be given the label with which you are happy.

### Should you bring your own accompanist?

For most festivals and competitions this will be expected, although some international competitions demand the use of the official pianist at the later stages. Some agents will also expect you to provide your own pianist, but many are geared to the opera-house system of providing an official accompanist. You may still bring your own pianist if you wish, and for you this is obviously an advantage: you can rehearse together, and there will be a friendly face behind the piano. Auditioning with your own pianist, however, does not show a panel how you react to singing without rehearsal, having to set a tempo for an unfamiliar pianist, pulling the accompanist on or back; also, the panel needs to see how easy or difficult it is for the official pianist to follow your rubato or coloratura. This is what it is looking out for: how you react to stress or to something which puts you off, and how strong you are in your musical, dramatic and vocal intentions. The panel doesn't worry too much if mistakes are made, or if you and the pianist are not always together.

In my experience as an accompanist, following good singers is no problem: they lead you through each phrase towards the next breath, and their tempo or pulse seems to come through their very bones. If the pianist stops playing during an aria, you should be able to carry on without the flicker of an eyelid. Your vocal line should be totally self-sufficient, without need of external support.

Thus, in many ways it is an advantage to use the official pianist. But make sure that your music is fully marked up with cuts, cadenzas, places where you take time, and any other signposts which will help the pianist to play as well as possible for you. Don't say too much to him or her before the audition; often a tempo given in the corridor is not related to the one needed on the stage. If the pianist plays the introduction too slowly or too fast, don't worry: just come in confidently and show the panel how it really goes. This makes a stronger impression than turning to the pianist and spitting out in a stage whisper – 'a bit faster!' If your whole body feels the correct tempo, even that vibration can be felt by a sensitive pianist who will then adjust to it.

The state of your music copy is also vital. If pages become separated or are torn out of the score in order to save weight, they are often handed to the pianist in the wrong order, or fall off the music stand and are impossible to turn. It is worth five minutes to bind them well. Sticking them in a scrapbook is often very helpful and practical. The type of folder where music can be slipped inside transparent pages, commonly used by American singers, is not so good; the pages are heavier to turn, and when light is reflected off the pages the music cannot be seen.

## What happens on the day?

Many people wake up with a feeling of apprehension and impending doom. Nerves can play havoc with your composure – don't let them. It is best to map out for yourself a schedule of things to do, leading up to the time of the audition, and then to approach the stages one by one. Keep yourself calm by concentrating on the small details of each action and try not to be rushed. This is no different from preparing for any performance – you are the most important person, so be in charge of yourself. Deep breathing and relaxation exercises can be a great help.

Your choice of clothes is obviously an individual matter. Wear something that is flattering and yet not showy. Make sure your shoes are comfortable and noiseless and that you have no distracting accessories. The panel may want to imagine you in costume, and this is made easier when your visual appearance is simple. Try to look tall if you are very small or plump, and solid if you are thin or lanky.

Aim to arrive in good time. This will enable you to settle down and get used to the atmosphere. Bear in mind that auditions are liable to run ahead of time. How you behave both before and after the audition is relevant: the impression you make upon the audition secretary who is organizing 'back stage' can be communicated to the panel, so be aware that you are already on show.

Your papers, which the panel members will have before them while you sing, are very important. Your curriculum vitae and publicity photograph are both vital to your success. Make sure they are concise and impeccably produced. The panel is always looking to discover more about you; help them all you can.

Once you have walked into the audition room, the way you announce your aria is a clue to your ability to speak on stage, so project your voice without shouting. Do not talk down to the panel by telling them something they already know; for example, do not say '"Dove sono", the

Countess's aria from *The Marriage of Figaro* by Mozart'. They know that *Figaro* is by Mozart; they know that 'Dove sono' is sung by the Countess. All you really need to say is '"Dove sono" from *Le nozze di Figaro*' and if they don't know what you mean, they can ask you. But tell them in what language you will be singing if it differs from the original or the usual version.

Should you act? The simple answer is yes, but with the voice. Imagine that you are recording and that the panel cannot see you. Every emotion and thought must be communicated through the voice, and physical gestures are only in addition to this. The panel needs to be able to imagine you in the role for which you are being considered, as well as in the one you are portraying. Acting is less a question of physical gesture or movement than of communication, and you must learn to register the effect of yourself at the back of the room or theatre, and respond to it.

**Being business-like**
Make sure that you have readily available at all times first class publicity photographs, up-to-date biographical details for inclusion in programmes, etc., and a clear, concise, current curriculum vitae. It is wise to spend some money on a good photograph by going to a professional photographer. You are looking for a well-lit head and shoulders portrait photograph that should flatter you without recourse to the 'Hollywood' glamour effect.

Biographical details do not fulfil the same role as a curriculum vitae. They need to be written in 'reported speech' and be flatteringly truthful. Any reviews that you have may be included, but should be restricted only to the important ones.

A curriculum vitae is a business document aimed at conveying information in a concise form. The panel may only have time to peruse your CV just before your audition, and you do not want panel members spending the precious moments while you sing engrossed in sorting out your papers. They need to be able to scan down a single page in order to pick out relevant details in which they are interested, and not find themselves reading an autobiography. Try not to use lengthy sentences such as 'I have continued my singing experience by singing in many different kinds of choirs both in and out of London (both professionally and non-professionally)'. Study the example for an explicit way of setting out the information.

Let us consider the various headings and the layout of your CV.

# Curriculum Vitae

**Name:** Use your professional name if it differs from your own.

**Date of Birth:** State this rather than your age – otherwise you will have to update your CV more frequently.

**Address:** Make sure this is an address at which you can be contacted, not the one from which you are just moving.

**Telephone/Fax/E-mail:** The same applies.

**Voice Type:** Be specific for German-speaking opera houses (see the section on the *Fach* system).

**Agent:** Only include this heading if you have one.

**Qualifications:** Use abbreviated form, e.g. 8 GCSE's; 3 A levels; ARCM. Don't spell them all out, subject by subject.

**Singing Teachers:** List chronologically.

**Operatic Roles:** Make these succinct, e.g. *Don Giovanni* (Company, Year).

**Oratorio:** As above.

**Recitals:** State venues/societies and dates, e.g. Wigmore Hall 2001.

**Masterclasses and Competitions:** Show classes under name of tutor, with dates, and list competitions, prizes won and dates.

**Future Engagements:** Only include this heading if you have any.

**Other Performing Experience:** List any other stage experience, e.g. straight theatre, film, television, and anything else which may be relevant.

**Referees:** These are not always needed. If they are, usually two are expected. Ensure that your nominated referees are agreeable to act for you, and that they are available for comment when contacted.

# The Art of French Song

19th and 20th Century Repertoire
Selected and Edited by Roger Nichols
Complete with translations and guidance on pronunciation

In each of these volumes the songs appear in the chronological order of their composer's birth, but Nichols somehow contrives a line-up of music which seems delightfully arbitrary at the same time as carefully designed to enrich everyone's understanding of the *mélodie*. The book also contains a remarkable amount of scholarship, lightly worn and pithily expressed. As well as complete translations of the songs, there is a useful and concise introduction on singing in French, together with an illuminating historical note and critical commentary; and Nichols gives full due to the poets who were of crucial importance in the development of the *mélodie* tradition. The editions champion French music in bringing this repertoire to new audiences, addressing the special needs of both English and German speakers in the translations and guidance on pronunciation and interpretation. All-in-all these books are indispensable to anyone with the same sense of delight and adventure that characterizes this wonderful repertoire – one of France's unsung, or at least under-sung, national treasures.

– Graham Johnson

| Volume 1 | | |
|---|---|---|
| High Voice: | EP7519a | £12.95 |
| Medium/Low Voice: | EP7519b | £12.95 |

The Art of French Song

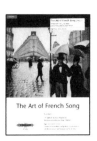

The Art of French Song

| Volume 2 | | |
|---|---|---|
| High Voice: | EP7520a | £12.95 |
| Medium/Low Voice: | EP7520b | £12.95 |

# Preparing your music

Preparation of music begins weeks before an audition and can be compared to an assault course. Each layer and detail of the music should be dealt with separately. One part of your brain looks after the words, the musical details, motivations and thought processes; another part looks after the singing, vowel sounds, emotions and imagination. This is a simplified explanation of the learning process, but it helps to know that the brain is divided into different compartments, which need to be programmed separately.

Let us start with the latter, the emotional compartment which deals with the singing. Emotions have to find their release in a physical outlet and, when someone is emotionally upset, one of these outlets is the human voice. In singing you are involved in communicating the emotions, thoughts and ideas of your chosen character. An aria or song can be the outpouring of great passion, as in 'Vissi d'arte' (Puccini's *Tosca*), or the highly articulate and verbal outpourings of Figaro in 'Largo al factotum' (Rossini's *Il barbiere di Siviglia*). If you have chosen an emotional aria, you run the risk of being dominated by those very emotions which you are trying to communicate, rather than being the master of them. Your breath and vocal cords (which work in tandem) are the first physical outlets which must be taught the music. Start by learning the notes: not just the tune, but each and every interval, so that the music becomes part of your very being.

The best way for a singer to approach this is to select his or her favourite and most comfortable (i.e. well-placed) vowel sound, and to sing the aria through on this sound alone, without at first being restricted by the rhythm, tempo and repeated notes of the piece. The voice needs to be taught the intervals and the shape of each phrase most thoroughly before going on to the next stage. If you sing your aria as a 'vocalise' with a perfect line and shape, you will then have a good foundation on which to build. Try to imagine which voice-sounds really carry through a hall. Not the short, cutting consonants (K's and G's) nor the plosives (P's, B's, T's) – but the open vowels. Any sustained note will have to be sung on a vowel sound, the consonants existing to give clarity, shape and meaning. It follows that any aria is made up of great stretches of vowel sounds, coloured and highlighted by the consonants.

When you are happy with this first part of the preparation and feel you understand the resonance and physical shape of each phrase, you can sing the aria with the vowels of the text. The addition of the original vowels will help to create the rhythm of the phrase. For example, let us take a phrase from 'O mio Fernando' (*La favorita* by Donizetti) sung by Leonora in Act III.

Assuming that you have already practised this on your favourite vowel sound and really know the intervals, move on to the next stage of putting the actual vowels in, which will look like this:

Some of the vowel sounds have caused certain notes to be tied together: for example, the C in bar 2 is tied over to the C in bar 3. Later, when you put in the consonants, the 'c' of 'come' will achieve the reiteration of the note, while you maintain the same vowel sound. This example represents, in a simplified form, an indication, through the vowel sounds, of the emotional content of the phrase.

A musical note can be sounded through certain voiced consonants, but the main job is done by the vowels. When looking for a word to express a feeling, often the shape of the vowel comes first into the mouth, before the word appears.

One way of thinking about this form of preparation is to organize the learning processes in the same order as the sound comes out of your body. The sound is first initiated by the breath, passes through the vocal cords and then is formed inside the mouth and the resonance chambers. Finally, the sound is projected out through the lips where the consonants are added.

Turning back to Example II, we can now add the consonants, which will provide some information about the reasons for the emotion.

The consonants are printed above the music to show how they are related to each vowel. Notice especially 'l'amor mio' where the end consonant of 'amor' is put together with the beginning consonant of 'mio'. This not only saves breath, but creates a smooth, flowing line. Some of the consonants can be sung, such as M, R, L, N, and these should be sung on the pitch of their respective following note, otherwise the effect on the listener is of bad intonation. Often when consonants are 'sung' on the wrong note or slide up to a note, you can be criticized for singing out of tune. Even the 'non-singing' consonants such as P, C, D, T should be imagined that they are sung on the correct note and you will often find that you can resonate a note on these consonants. Consonants are often forgotten about or treated as a nuisance in singing lessons and yet they can be angels in disguise and be extraordinarily expressive. Even in a different context, such as a patter song, with a less legato phrase, it is still worth teaching the voice the music in this bel canto way. The vocal line, once assured and with the tone of the voice threading its way through the phrase, can always be broken up later.

It is worth pointing out that the expression mark >, so commonly used in bel canto music over certain melodic notes (as, for instance, in Example I), does not mean *sforzando* or an accent on the word as in 20th-century music. The note is important for the tessitura of the phrase, and should be sung long with a certain weight of sound. The notation > comes from a shorthand version of the sign for a *messa di voce*: <>. Accenting these notes can cause your voice to tire quickly, and many bel canto operas have a plethora of these signs (although vocal and full scores often differ in the placing of them). The other sign is the 'cap-accent' or 'smorzatura' which indicates a *sforzando* kind of accent, though, as in the following example, the syllable should not be over-accented because this can often produce incorrect stresses. Here is an example demonstrating the two signs for tenuto and accent, from

Violetta's aria 'Addio, del passato' in Act III of Verdi's *La traviata*. The preparation of that part of your brain which deals with the intellectual side consists of establishing the correct pronunciation of the words on a declamatory level, the understanding of their full meaning, and the appreciation of the motivations of the character within the drama. All this work can be done without singing, away from the piano, but can, of course, be happening at the same time as the other learning process.

It is vital to start by checking your edition of the music. Many albums contain strange versions of arias or songs, sometimes in the wrong key, or badly arranged and inaccurate. If you can, go to a library and check your music against a recognized edition, otherwise you may have to relearn that aria when you come to sing the whole work. Most arias and songs will be in a foreign language, so make sure that your use of that language is as perfect as possible. If you only understand the general sense of a phrase, you can only draw a sketch of the meaning, but if you know the meaning of every word, you can paint a picture with as much detail as you like. The sound and timbre of the language all add greatly to the resonance of your voice. Imagine you have to go on stage and speak the text at its own natural pace and rhythm, and then try to slow the words to the tempo of the music, and shape the words into the rhythm of the vocal line. You will generally find that composers' settings are slower than natural speech, and the singer must find a way to sound the words at this slower pace. Let us take another example from 'O mio Fernando'. Speak the words in the recitative at a natural speed, allowing your own gaps between phrases:

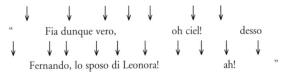

When you have experimented with this for a while, try the phrase in Donizetti's tempo:

Once you experiment with this, you can begin to understand how Donizetti creates a feeling of agitation in the text. Stanislavsky talked about tempo and rhythm of acting in relation to opera: 'In opera the rhythm is there, and all there is left for you to do is to be clear in your minds why the composer wrote your aria in 3/4 time and not in 6/8 time, and why he has made these and not those words operative ones. Once you have realized that, your task is clear: to adapt your physical and psychological data to the ready-made rhythm of the composer' (*Stanislavsky on The Art of the Stage*, Faber & Faber, 1950).

The natural intonation of the words must be preserved in spite of the written melodic notes, which often serve the emotional content of the text. Try another experiment by singing the text in rhythm on one comfortable note in your range, rather like an emotional cantor in church:

When the orchestral or piano accompaniment is not rhythmical, or even silent, the vocal rhythm may become more fluid and natural if so desired, but without losing the organic inner sense of the rhythm.

Your singing should encapsulate the total dramatic vision of the composer. It is not a replacement for the text. The composer began with only the text in front of him and had to imbue this with his vision of the drama *before* writing the music. How would *you* set the words? In the end, the composer's setting must become yours. The projection of the music comes both through the singing and through the words. The resonance of words and singing when combined must always add up to 100%. Bear in mind that most situations that happen in opera could only occur once in anybody's life, so treat them in that way – amazing cathartic experiences to which your body reacts, through your voice, the music and the text. In real life you sometimes need to speak very clearly, as when giving out important information. At other times you may be emotionally upset and you will find yourself speaking indistinctly with more vowels than consonants. You have to decide how much information the audience needs to know about why you are emotionally upset. The balance between words and music has been a continual question over the ages and the problem will never be solved for you: you can only solve it for yourself. In a recitative, it could be 30% voice, 70% text; in a lyrical melody, 60% voice, 40% text.

Having thus considered the two facets of the learning process, combining them will be enormously exciting. Finally, the way you perform the aria will be in response to the various stimuli around you: the acoustics of the hall, the atmosphere of the audition, and your own desire to communicate.

Keep going back to fundamental points. Ask yourself what you are best at communicating, what suits your voice, personality and looks. In opera, know what the entire role entails, not just the aria. Having satisfied yourself that this is truly your best role, remember that the panel arrives at an audition hoping that this will be their lucky day, the day when they will find the magic singer. They want you to be the best, to sing the best, to look the best. Remember that they are on your side!

# Festivals and competitions

**The competitive festival**

There are many festivals and eisteddfodau all over Great Britain and a list of these can be found in the *British Music Education Yearbook* (Rhinegold Publishing, annually). Normally, singers choose to enter local competitive events. These give all participants the experience of performing before a panel of friendly judges who will usually write a helpful critical report as well as giving a placing within the event. This is one of the best ways for a singer to receive an unprejudiced opinion of what comes across to an audience from his or her performance. The more times a singer stands up before an audience, the more this initially frightening experience will become as natural as breathing. Enjoy the music, the text and the meaning, and communicate that enjoyment. Many times, a singer in the audience has been inspired by just such a performance to rush out and buy the song the next day.

**The singing competition**

If you find that you are no longer challenged by the standard of a festival, you may choose to enter a singing competition.

The approach to the technique of singing in competitions is more akin to performing than to auditioning. By the time you reach the finals, after filling in the application form, singing in the first round, and (usually some months later) singing in the semi-finals, you will have a pretty good idea of what the panel expects. The brochure will list the arias from which you can choose, and will often state the qualities that the panel will be looking for. For instance, the Rosa Ponselle Competition once stated as its judging criteria:

1 *Quality of voice*
2 *Vocal technique* (a) mask resonance, (b) relaxed, low larynx,

    (c) relaxed jaw, (d) full development of each vocal register, meshing
    into a seamless and even scale, (e) low breath support, (f) correctly sup-
    ported *pianissimo*, (g) correct trill, (h) legato line, (i) agility, (j) staccato.
3 *Musicality*
4 *Intonation*
5 *Artistic interpretation*
6 *Language facility*
7 *Articulation of words*
8 *Stage presence and deportment*

It is in the nature of competitions that the best performers usually win,
notwithstanding the usefulness of their voices; the choice of brilliant
arias is obviously an advantage. The benefits for young singers in entering competitions are not only the chances of winning prizes and the
honours attached, but also the public exposure in concerts or opera.
Even if you do not win, someone on the panel or in the audience may
help you in your career, and many singers have made their break in this
way. Often there are representatives from music societies, opera companies and orchestras present who are searching for new talent. Another
advantage is the always-valuable opportunity of performing in public,
albeit not in ideal circumstances, but 'normal' performing will seem so
much easier in comparison. The singer who wins may quickly get too
much exposure and may not be able to cope with all the highly pressurized commitments which result from winning first prize.

  Disadvantages of entering competitions may include a possible nega-
tive reaction to the competitive atmosphere backstage, and the enor-
mous danger of trying too hard while performing. Your arias will have
been chosen months before, and you may subsequently be unhappy
with your choice and find that you cannot change it. However, a
Wigmore Hall recital also has to be programmed months in advance, so
there is little difference. Moreover, it is often the case that, by chance,
the contestant before you sings in a brilliant fashion exactly the same
arias as you have chosen.

  Competitions can be very unpleasant affairs, but you will learn to
adopt a philosophical attitude towards performing. Find a way simply to
enjoy singing, to enjoy the music that you are singing, and to let nothing invade on this. You can only communicate what you have to give, so
accept this, and communicate wholeheartedly and with enjoyment.

# UK singing competitions

**Bayreuth Bursary Competition**
(young Wagnerian singers,
maximum age 35; January)
Administrator: Roger Temple
c/o The Wagner Society, 45
Frankfield Rise, Tunbridge Wells,
Kent TN2 5LF
ⓣ 01892 539781

**Kathleen Ferrier Memorial
Scholarship Competition**
(British singers, age 21–28; April)
Administrator: Shirley Barr
52 Rosebank, Holyport Road,
London SW6 6LY
ⓣ 020 7381 0985
ⓔ www:ferrierawards.org.uk

**National Mozart Competition**
(maximum age 33; December)
Administrator: Barbara Dix
66 Talpot Street, Southport,
Merseyside PR8 1LU
ⓣ / ⓕ 01704 530903

**Royal Over-Seas League
Music Competitions**
(several prizes for Commonwealth
and past Commonwealth singers;
maximum age 30; Feb–April)
Administrator: Roderick Lakin
Royal Over-Seas League, Park Place,
St James's, London SW1A 1LR
ⓣ 020 7408 0214 Ext 219
ⓕ 020 7499 6738
ⓔ culture@rosl.org.uk

**South East Arts Musicians' Platform**
(maximum age 30; May)
Administrator: Deborah Rees
19 Bourne Road, London N8 9HJ
ⓣ 020 8340 4116
ⓕ 020 8348 8894

**Richard Tauber Prize**
(open to British and Austrian
singers; age, men 21–32, women
21–30; biennial, even-numbered
years; spring)
Administrator: Tony Fessler
Anglo-Austrian Music Society,
46 Queen Anne's Gate,
London SW1H 9AU
ⓣ 020 7222 0366
ⓕ 020 7233 0293

**Maggie Teyte/Miriam
Licette Awards**
(female singers, maximum
age 30; January)
Administrator: Felicity Guinness
2 Keats Grove, London NW3 2RT
ⓣ 020 7435 5861
ⓕ 020 7431 5706

**Wigmore Hall International
Song Competition**
(Maximum age 32; September)
Administrator: Virginia Harding
Room 609, Langham House, 308
Regent Street, London W1R 5AL
ⓣ 020 7637 8515
ⓕ 020 7637 8516
ⓔ whisc@compuserve.com

# Main international singing competitions

All listed in the Fédération Mondiale des Concours Internationaux de Musique available from: 104 rue de Carouge, CH-1205 Genève, Switzerland
ⓣ +41 22 321 3260
ⓕ +41 22 781 1418
ⓔ fmcim@iprolink.ch

## Austria

### International Belvedere Hans Gabor Competition for Opera Singers

(maximum age, men under 32, women under 30; July)
Administrator: Isabella Gabor
Fleischmarkt 24,
A-1010 Wien, Austria
ⓣ +43 1 512 0100
ⓕ +43 1 512 010020
Email: wienerkammeroper@magnet.at

## Belgium

### International Singing Contest

(age, men 18–35, women 18–30; biennial, odd-numbered years; May)
Administrator: Cécile Duvivier
c/o Opera Royal de Wallonie,
rue des Dominicains 1,
B-4000 Liège, Belgium
ⓣ +32 41 221 4720
ⓕ +32 41 210201
ⓔ direction@orw.be

### Queen Elizabeth International Music Competition of Belgium

(not every year for singers; May)
Administrator: Cécile Ferrière
20 rue aux Laines,

B-1000 Bruxelles, Belgium
ⓣ +32 25 130099
ⓕ +32 25 143297
ⓔ info@concours-reine-elisabeth.be

## Czech Republic

### Emma Destinn International Singing Competition

(maximum age 35; August)
Administrator: Antonín Kazil
Rudolfov 393, CR-373 71
Ceske Budejovice, Czech Republic
ⓣ / ⓕ +420 383 9254

### International Singing Contest of Antonín Dvořák

(maximum age, men under 32, women under 30; November)
Administrator: Marie Drlíková
KC Amethyst, I P Pavlova 14,
CR-360 01 Karlovy Vary,
Czech Republic
ⓣ +420 17 322 8707/8
ⓕ +420 17 322 3753

## France

### International Singing and Chamber Music Competition

(maximum age, men 34, women 32; biennial, even-numbered years; June/July)
Administrator: Christiane de Bayser
Secrétariat, 8 rue du Dôme,
F-75116 Paris, France
ⓣ +33 1 47 047638
ⓕ +33 1 47 273503
ⓔ ufam@wanadoo.fr

### Toulouse International Voice Competition

(maximum age 33; biennial, even-numbered years; September)
Administrator: George Canet

Théâtre du Capitole, F-31000
Toulouse, France
ⓣ +33 5 61 621351
ⓕ +33 5 61 629690

# Germany

### Carl Orff International Singing Competition
(maximum age 33, not mezzos; June)
Carl Orff-Stiftung, Herzogstrasse 57,
D-80803 München, Germany
ⓣ +49 89 335033
ⓕ +49 89 335937
ⓔ carlorffst@aol.com

### Cologne International Singing Competition
(maximum age 30;
September/October 2002)
Administrator: Gerhard Peters
The Helga and Paul Hohnen
Foundation, Dagobertstrasse 38,
D-50668 Köln, Germany
ⓣ +49 221 912 818112
ⓕ +49 221 912 131204
ⓔ barbara.schmidt@uni-koeln.de

### International Music Competition of the ARD
(age, men 20–32, women
20–30; September)
Administrator: Renate Ronnefeld
Bayerischer Rundfunk,
D-80300 München, Germany
ⓣ +49 895 900 2471
ⓕ +49 895 900 3091
ⓔ ard.conc@br-mail.de

### International Singers' Contest 'Alexander Girardi'
(age, men 18–32, women 18–30;
June/July 2001)
Administrator: Albrecht Tauer

Kulturabteilung der Stadt Coburg,
Steingasse 18, D-96450 Coburg,
Germany
ⓣ +49 956 189 1402
ⓕ +49 956 189 1029

### International Singing Contest 'New Voices'
(maximum age, men 32, women
30; biennial, odd-numbered years;
autumn)
Administrator: Nadine Lindemann
Carl-Bertelsmann-Strasse 256,
PO Box 103, D-33311 Gütersloh,
Germany
ⓣ +49 524 181 7372
ⓕ +49 524 181 9513
ⓔ nadine.lindemann@bertelsmann.de

# Greece

### Maria Callas Grand Prix for Singers
(maximum age, men 32, women 30;
biennial, odd-numbered years; Spring)
Administrator: Anna Koukouraki
Athenaeum International Cultural
Centre, 3 Adrianou Street,
GR-105 55 Athens, Greece
ⓣ +30 1 321 1949
ⓕ +30 1 321 1196
ⓔ athenm@ibm.net

# Italy

### Bellini International Voice Competition
(no age limit; June/July)
Administrator: Salvatore Moltisanti
Ibla International Music Foundation,
226 E. Second Street, Suite 5D,
New York, NY10019, USA
ⓣ +1 212 387 0111
ⓕ +1 212 388 0102

**Competition for Young Opera Singers belonging to the European Community**

(maximum age, sopranos/tenors 30, others 32; March)
Administrator: Lapore Claudio
Istituzione Teatro Lirico
Sperimentale, di Spoleto 'A Belli',
Piazza G. Bovio 1, I-06049
Spoleto (PG), Italy
ⓉＴ +39 0743 221645
Ｆ +39 0743 222930
Ｅ teatrolirico@mail.caribusiness.it

**Toti dal Monte International Singing Competition** (July)

Administrator: Lucio de Piccoli
Ente Teatro Communale,
Corso del Popolo 31, via Diaz 7,
I-31100 Treviso, Italy
Ｔ +39 0422 410130
Ｆ +39 0422 582285

## Netherlands

**International Vocal Competition**

(maximum age 30; September)
Administrator: Arthur Oostvogel
PO Box 1225, NL-5200 BG
'sHertogenbosch, Netherlands
Ｔ +31 73 690 0999
Ｆ +31 73 690 1166

## Poland

**Stanisław Moniuszko Vocal Competition**

(maximum age 35; Triennial)
Administrator: Maria Foltyn
Plac Teatralny 1, PL-00950
Warszawa, Poland
Ｔ +48 22 692 0642
Ｆ +48 22 692 0742

## Spain

**Francisco Vinas International Singing Contest**

(maximum age, men 35,
women 32; January)
Administrator: Maria Vilardell
Vinas Calle Bruc 125, E-08037
Barcelona, Spain
Ｔ +34 932 154227
Ｆ +34 934 578646

**International Singing Competition Alfredo Kraus**

(age, men 20–35, women 18–32;
biennial, odd-numbered years)
Administrator: Juan Antonio
González Ojellón
Bravo Murillo 21–23, E-35003
Las Palmas de Gran Canaria, Spain
Ｔ +34 928 320513
Ｆ +34 928 314747
Ｅ orfigc@orfigc.com

**Julian Gayarre International Singing Competition**

(maximum age, men 35,
women 32; biennial, even-
numbered years; September)
Administrator: Ignacio Aranaz
Calle Santo Domingo 6,
E-31001 Pamplona, Spain
Ｔ +34 948 426072
Ｆ +34 948 223906
Ｅ iaranazz@cfnavarra.es

**Maria Canals International Competition for Musical Performance** (age 18–35; April)

Administrator: Elisabeth Martinez
Gran Via de les Corts Catalanes 654,
E-08010 Barcelona, Spain
Ｔ / Ｆ +34 93 318 7731

# USA

**Florida Grand Opera Young Artist Studio and Technical Apprentice Programs**
(December)
1200 Coral Way, Miami, FL
33145/2980, USA
ⓣ +1 305 854 1643
ⓕ +1 305 856 1042
ⓔ info@fgo.org

**Friedrich Schorr Memorial Performance Prize in Voice**
Administrator: David Katz
110 S. Madison Street, Adrian,
MI 49221-2575, USA
ⓣ +1 517 264 3121
ⓕ +1 517 265 3607

**Loren L. Zachery Society National Vocal Competition for Young Opera Singers**
(age, men 21–35, women 21–33;
March/April)
Administrator: Nedra Zachery
2250 Gloaming Way, Beverly Hills,
CA 90210, USA
ⓣ +1 310 276 2731
ⓕ +1 310 275 8245

**Marguerite McCammon Voice Competition**
(age, men 21–35, women 21–32;
biennial, odd-numbered years)
Administrator: Pat Crowley
Opera Guild of Fort Worth,
PO Box 100381, Fort Worth,
TX 76185-0381, USA
ⓣ +1 817 924 1536
ⓕ +1 817 924 1886
ⓔ geopat@ftw.com

# Vocal Duets

Bizet   Au fond du temple saint
Duet from *The Pearl Fishers*
Tenor, Baritone & Piano
Edited by Roger Nichols
EP 7588   £3.95

Significantly, this new edition presents the singers with two versions of the ever-popular duet. Not only do we include a superior edition of the well-known version, made by Bizet's publisher, Choudens, after his death, but also Bizet's original version, which has been unjustly neglected since the première of the opera in 1863.

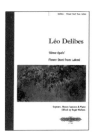

Delibes   Dôme épais
Flower Duet from *Lakmé*
Soprano, Mezzo-Soprano & Piano
Edited by Roger Nichols
EP 7589   £3.95

'[Lakmé] is set in a province of nineteenth-century India under British rule, and the opening scene, during which this duet is heard, takes place in the beautiful garden of the temple built by the Brahmin priest, Nilakantha. He hates the British invaders (for one thing, they have forbidden him to practise his religion) and the plot hinges around the clash between this hatred and the love between his daughter Lakmé and the British officer Gérald. Before Gérald appears, Lakmé and her slave Mallika sing this duet as they prepare to bathe in the river.'

# Opera auditions

Within the United Kingdom there are at present five full-time opera companies and many seasonal ones, which are listed below. On the continent there are many more, with the greatest number of these concentrated within the German-speaking countries. The process of applying to the German-speaking companies is unique and is dealt with in depth later. All other opera companies within such countries as the Netherlands, France, Spain, Italy, Scandinavia, America and Australia can be approached in much the same way as those in the UK.

Should you speak their language? Of course this is helpful, but if you do not, don't be put off: try and attempt the language in order to show your willingness to learn. Often you will discover that the panel members speak English better than you expect. They will require you to sing at least one aria in their language to enable you to demonstrate your diction and pronunciation.

### Auditioning in the UK and non-German-speaking countries

The usual practice is to apply either through an agent or directly to the respective opera house. A list of opera companies relevant to this section, together with the main British opera agents, is given below.

If agents have time to hear you and need your type of voice on their books, they will usually be prepared to work for you. They will know about vacancies in casting within opera houses, but more through word of mouth than through any organized system. The more established agents will have better knowledge and stronger contacts. As already mentioned, you can apply directly to an opera house, but they will expect an agent to negotiate your contract, and having an agent will help towards easier relations with the company.

### Auditioning for an agent

When writing to agents, give them as much information as you can: biographical details and work experience, repertoire, future engagements and a good photograph. Unless they have already heard of you, you must encourage them to take an interest in you by marketing yourself well. (Note the section on 'Being business-like' on pages 16–17.) If you have an impending performance in the locality, invite them to attend, providing complimentary tickets. If they can't hear you in performance, they may ask you to audition and will not only expect to hear opera, but also oratorio and song. They will be interested in all your capabilities, which can generate work both for you and for them. An agency is only as good as its clients.

### Auditioning for an opera company

If you are contacting an opera company direct, you should write to the Audition Secretary, unless you have a contact already. Your letter should include the same information as for an agent with, again, details of any impending performances, sending complimentary tickets – opera companies often send someone to talent-spot at performances. The company may hold auditions at any time of the year, either at regular intervals or when the number of applicants reaches a certain level. Sometimes an audition can be set up at short notice either through an agent or because the company is interested in your credentials.

Normally, an opera company will first hear you in a hall or room before asking you to return for a stage audition. Your appointed time will mean what it says, but there may be the inevitable delay, or the panel may be ahead of time due to last minute cancellations. Do not feel pressurized to sing before your appointed time if you feel you are not ready: just quietly inform them that you would prefer to wait.

The stage audition can be a strange experience, often tense and hurried; the dusty upright piano might be on the side of the stage or in the wings, or even in the orchestra pit where you can hardly hear it. You wonder how to pass your music down to the pianist in the darkness below. A common time for these auditions is around 6 p.m., after the stage technicians have finished building the set and before the evening performance. Some sets are better than others for resonance; thick curtains on the set, for example, will tend to soak up the sound. Offstage noises, such as hammering, are common at quiet moments in the music.

Ushers will also be heard discussing their latest bargain in clear, projected tones from high in the balcony. The reaction from the panel to your singing may be no more than the words 'thank you' (with all their subtle intonations and meanings), but do not be upset. There was a famous incident when auditions were held in an old London theatre for a musical. Hundreds of young hopefuls arrived. Just before one of them was due to go on stage, the stage manager asked a stagehand to close a skylight. The stage manager first introduced the auditionee from the stage to the panel, and then looked up to the flies to see if the skylight was closed, shouting 'thank you', whereupon the auditionee disappeared. She had been rejected so often that the words had a magic power.

# Main UK opera agents

**Allied Artists**
42 Montpelier Square,
London SW7 1JZ
ⓣ 020 7589 6243
ⓕ 020 7581 5269

**Askonas Holt Ltd**
Lonsdale Chambers, 27 Chancery
Lane, London WC2A 1PF
ⓣ 020 7400 1700
ⓕ 020 7400 1799

**Clarion/Seven Muses**
47 Whitehall Park,
London N19 3TW
ⓣ 020 7272 4413
ⓕ 020 7281 9687

**Connaught Artists Management**
2 Molasses Row, Plantation Wharf,
London SW11 3UX
ⓣ 020 7738 0017
ⓕ 07070 603710

**C. & M. Craig Services**
11 Henning Street, Battersea,
London SW11 3DR
ⓣ 020 7228 4855
ⓕ 020 7223 2189

**Karen Durant Management**
298 Nelson Road, Whitton,
Middlesex TW2 7BW
ⓣ 020 8893 3172
ⓕ 020 8893 8090

**Robert Gilder & Co.**
Enterprise House, 59–65 Upper
Ground, London SE1 9PQ
ⓣ 020 7928 9008
ⓕ 020 7928 9755

**Patricia Greenan**
19B Belsize Park,
London NW3 4SF
ⓣ 020 7794 5954
ⓕ 020 7431 3503

**Harlequin Promotions**
203 Fidlas Road,
Cardiff CF1 45NA
ⓣ 01222 750821
ⓕ 01222 755971

**Harrison/Parrott Ltd**
12 Penzance Place, London W11 4PA
ⓣ 020 7229 9166
ⓕ 020 7221 5042

**Hazard Chase Ltd**
Norman House, Cambridge Place,
Cambridge CB2 1NS
ⓣ 01223 312400
ⓕ 01223 460827

**ICM Artists**
Oxford House, 76 Oxford Street,
London W1N 0AX
ⓣ 020 7636 6565
ⓕ 020 7323 0101

**IMG Artists**
Lovell House,
616 Chiswick High Road,
London W4 5RX
ⓣ 020 8233 5800
ⓕ 020 8742 8758

**Ingpen and Williams**
26 Wadham Road,
London SW15 2LR
ⓣ 020 8874 3222
ⓕ 020 8877 3113

**Sue Lubbock Artist Management**
25 Courthorpe Road,
London NW3 2LE
ⓣ 020 7485 5932
ⓕ 020 7267 0179

**Penelope Marland Artists
Management**
10 Roseneath Road,
London SW11 6AH
ⓣ 020 7223 7319
ⓕ 020 7771 0675

**Music International**
13 Ardilaun Road, London N5 2QR
ⓣ 020 7359 5183
ⓕ 020 7226 9792

**Musicmakers**
Tailor House, 63–65 High Street,
Whitwell, Herts. SG4 8AH
ⓣ 01438 871708
ⓕ 01483 871777

**Opera & Concert Artists**
75 Aberdare Gardens,
London NW6 3AN
ⓣ 020 7328 3097
ⓕ 020 7372 3537

**Owen/White Management**
Top Floor 59 Lansdowne Place,
Hove, E. Sussex BN3 1FL
ⓣ 01273 727127
ⓕ 01273 328128

**Performing Arts**
6 Windmill Street,
London W1P 1HF
ⓣ 020 7255 1362
ⓕ 020 7631 4631

**Caroline Phillips Management**
Tailor House, 63–65 High Street,
Whitwell, Herts. SG4 8AH
ⓣ 01483 871828
ⓕ 01483 871838

**Phoenix Artist Management**
4th Floor, 6 Windmill Street,
London W1P 1HF
ⓣ 020 7636 5021
ⓕ 020 7631 4631

**Antony Pristavec Artist &
Concert Management**
79 Norbury Crescent,
London SW16 4JT
ⓣ 020 8679 0369
ⓕ 020 8679 9399

**Mark Riches Personal
Management**
59 Kendall Avenue South,
Sanderstead, Surrey CR2 0QR
ⓣ / ⓕ 020 8660 2443

**Stafford Law**
6 Barham Close, Weybridge,
Surrey KT13 9PR
ⓣ 01932 854 489
ⓕ 01932 858 521

**Athole Still**
Foresters Hall, 25–27 Westow
Street, London SE19 3RY
ⓣ 020 8771 5271
ⓕ 020 8771 8172

**Helen Sykes Artists' Management**
100 Felsham Road, Putney,
London SW15 1DQ
ⓣ 020 8780 0060
ⓕ 020 8780 8772

**Van Walsum Management**
4 Addison Bridge Place,
London W14 8XP
ⓣ 020 7371 4343
ⓕ 020 7371 4344

**Patrick Voullaire**
Park Offices, 121 Dora Road,
London SW19 7JT
ⓣ 020 8946 8848
ⓕ 020 8944 1317

**Young Concert Artists Trust**
23 Garrick Street,
London WC2E 9AX
ⓣ 020 7379 8477
ⓕ 020 7379 8467

# UK opera companies
(full-time)

**English National Opera**
(ⓣ 020 7836 0111)
London Coliseum, St Martin's Lane,
London WC2N 4ES

**Opera North**
(ⓣ 0113 243 9999)
Grand Theatre, 46 New Briggate,
Leeds LS1 6NU

**The Royal Opera**
(ⓣ 020 7240 1200)
Royal Opera House, Covent Garden,
London WC2E 9DD

**Scottish Opera**
(ⓣ 0141 248 4567)
39 Elmbank Cresent,
Glasgow G2 4PT

**Welsh National Opera**
(ⓣ 029 2046 4666)
John Street, Cardiff CFl 4SP

# UK opera companies
(part-time)

**Almeida Opera**
(ⓣ 020 7226 7432)
Almeida Theatre, Almeida Street,
London N1 1TA

**Birmingham Opera Company**
(ⓣ 0121 246 6644)
205 The Argent Centre,
60 Frederick Street,
Birmingham B1 3HS

**Broomhill Opera**
(ⓣ 020 7702 9555)
Wilton's Music Hall,
1 Grace's Alley, Wellclose Square,
London E1 8JB

**Camberwell Pocket Opera**
(ⓣ 020 7635 8905)
19 Nigel Road, London SE15 4NP

**Castleward Opera**
(ⓣ 028 9066 1090)
737 Lisburn Road, Belfast,
N. Ireland

**Central Festival Opera Ltd**
(ⓣ 01604 233082)
411B Wellingborough Road,
Abington, Northampton NN1 4EY

**Court Opera Productions**
(ⓣ 01305 264420)
Durngate House, 3 Durngate Street,
Dorchester, Dorset DT1 1JP

**Crystal Clear Opera**
(ⓣ 01480 810261)
The Old Rectory, Grafham,
Cambs. PE18 0BB

**D'Oyly Carte Opera Company**
(ⓣ 020 7793 7100)
The Powerhouse, 6 Sancroft Street,
London SE11 5UD

**Diva Opera**
(ⓣ 020 8932 8555)
115 Princes Gardens, London W3 0LR

**Dorset Opera**
(ⓣ 01202 481856)
13 The Stables, Dragoon Way,
Christchurch, Dorset BH23 2TY

**English Touring Opera**
(ⓣ 020 7820 1131)
250A Kennington Lane,
London SE11 5RD

**European Chamber Opera**
(ⓣ 020 8806 4231)
60C Kyverdale Road,
London N16 7AJ

**Garsington Opera Ltd**
(ⓣ 01865 368201)
Garsington Manor, Garsington,
Oxford OX44 9DH

**Glyndebourne Festival and
Touring Opera**
(ⓣ 01273 812321)
Glyndebourne, Lewes,
Sussex BN8 5UU

**Grange Park Opera**
(ⓣ 020 7246 7567)
1 Fleet Place, London EC4M 7WS

**London Opera Players**
(ⓣ 01483 81004)
Broadmeade Copse, Westwood Lane,
Wanborough, Surrey GU3 2JN

**Mid Wales Opera**
(ⓣ 01938 500611)
Meifod, Powys SY22 6BY

**Opera Box Ltd**
(ⓣ 01874 690339)
Rhydyberi Cottages, Merthyr Cynog,
Brecon, Powys LD3 9SA

**Opera Brava**
(ⓣ 01444 443060)
67 Franklynn Road, Haywards Heath,
W Sussex RH16 4DT

**Opera Holland Park**
(ⓣ 020 7361 3058)
Central Library, Phillimore Walk,
London W8 7RX

**Pavilion Opera**
(ⓣ 01526 378231)
Thorpe Tilney Hall, Thorpe Tilney,
Nr Lincoln, LN4 3SL

# Main European opera companies
(non-German-speaking)

## Belgium
**De Vlaamse Opera**
Van Ertbornstraat 8, B-2018
Antwerpen, Belgium

**L'Opéra Royal de Wallonie**
rue des Dominicains 1, B-4000
Liege, Belgium

**Théâtre Royal de la Monnaie**
Koninklijke Muntschouwburg,
rue Leopoldstraat 4, B-1000
Bruxelles, Belgium

# Denmark
**Den Jyske Opera**
Musikhuset Aarhus, Thomas Jensens
Allé, DK-8000 Aarhus C, Denmark

**The Royal Danish Opera**
The Royal Theatre, PO Box 2185,
DK-1017 Copenhagen K, Denmark

# Finland
**Finnish National Opera**
PO Box 176, Helsinginkatu 58,
FIN-00251 Helsinki, Finland

# France
**Châtelet Théâtre Musical**
2 rue Edouard Colonne,
F-75001 Paris, France

**Opéra Bastille**
11 bis avenue Daumesnil,
F-75012 Paris, France

**L'Opéra Comique**
5 rue Favart, F-75002 Paris, France

**L'Opéra de Nancy et de Lorraine**
1 rue Sainte-Catherine,
F-54000 Nancy, France

**Opéra de Lyon**
1 place de la Comédie,
F-69001 Lyon, France

**Opéra de Nice**
4 rue St François de Paule,
F-06000 Nice, France

**L'Opéra de Lille**
2 rue des Bons Enfants,
F-59800 Lille, France

**Opéra National du Rhin**
19 place Broglie, BP 320,
F-67008 Strasbourg Cedex, France

**Théâtre des Champs Elysées**
15 avenue Montaigne,
F-75008 Paris, France

# Greece
**Greek National Opera**
18 Charilaou Tricoupi,
GR-106 79 Athens, Greece

# Iceland
**Islenska Operan**
Gamla Bio, Ingolfsstraeti, PO Box
1416, 121 Reykjavik, Iceland

# Ireland
**Opera Ireland**
John Player House,
276–288 South Circular Road,
Dublin 8, Republic of Ireland

# Israel
**New Israel Opera**
Tel Aviv Performing Arts Centre,
28 Leonardo da Vinci, PO Box
33321, Tel Aviv 61332, Israel

# Italy
**Teatro Comunale
'G.Verdi' di Trieste**
Riva 3 Novembre 1,
I-34121 Trieste, Italy

**Teatro Comunale di Bologna**
Largo Respighi 1,
I-40126 Bologna, Italy

**Teatro Comunale di Firenze**
Via Solferino 15,
I-50123 Firenze, Italy

**Teatro Alla Scala di Milano**
Via Filodrammatici 2,
I-20121 Milano, Italy

**Teatro di San Carlo di Napoli**
Via San Carlo, 98 F,
I-80132 Napoli, Italy

**Teatro Massimo di Palermo**
Via R. Wagner 2,
I-90139 Palermo, Italy

**Teatro dell'Opera di Roma**
Piazza B. Gigli 8,
I-00184 Roma, Italy

**Teatro Regio di Torino**
Piazza Castello 215,
I-10124 Torino, Italy

## Monaco
**L'Opéra de Monte-Carlo**
Place du Casino, BP 139, MC-98007 Monte Carlo, Monaco

## Netherlands
**National Reisopera**
Perikweg 97, Postbus 1321,
NL-7512 DP Enschede, Netherlands

**De Nederlandse Opera**
Waterlooplein 22, NL-1011 PG
Amsterdam, Netherlands

**Opera Zuid**
Postbus 104, NL-6200 AC
Maastricht, Netherlands

## Norway
**Den Norske Opera**
Box 8800, Youngstorget, N-0028
Oslo, Norway

## Portugal
**Fundacao de Opera de
Teatro Sao Carlos**
Rua Serpa Pinto 9,
P-1200 Lisbon, Portugal

## Spain
**Gran Teatro del Lices**
Sant Pau, Barcelona, Spain

## Sweden
**Drottingholms Slottsteater**
PO Box 270500, S-10251
Stockholm, Sweden

**Royal Swedish Opera**
Vastra Tradardsgatan 2, Box 160 94,
S-103 22 Stockholm, Sweden

# Main American opera companies

## Arizona
**Arizona Opera**
3501 North Mountain Ave, Tucson,
AZ 85719, USA

## California
**Los Angeles Music Centre Opera**
135 N. Grand Avenue, Los Angeles,
CA 90012, USA

**San Francisco Opera**
War Memorial Opera House, San
Francisco, CA 94012-4509, USA

**San Diego Opera**
18th Floor Civic Centre Plaza, 1200
Third Avenue, San Diego, CA
92101-4112, USA

# District of Columbia
**The Washington Opera**
2600 Virginia Avenue, NW, Suite
104, Washington, DC 20037, USA

# Florida
**Florida Grand Opera**
1200 Coral Way, Miami,
FL 33145-2980, USA

# Illinois
**Lyric Opera of Chicago**
20 North Wacker Drive, Chicago,
IL 60606, USA

# Kentucky
**Kentucky Opera**
101 S. Eighth Street, Louisville,
KY 40202-4016, USA

# Louisiana
**New Orleans Opera Association**
305 Baronne Street, Suite 500,
New Orleans, LA 70112-1618, USA

# Maryland
**Baltimore Opera Company**
110 W. Mount Royal Avenue,
Suite 306, Baltimore,
MD 21201-5030, USA

# Michigan
**Michigan Opera Theatre**
Lothrop Landing,
104 Lothrop, Detroit,
MI 48202, USA

# Minnesota
**The Minnesota Opera**
620 North First Street, Minneapolis,
MN 55401, USA

# Missouri
**Opera Theatre of Saint Louis**
PO Box 191910, St Louis,
MO 63119-7910, USA

# New Mexico
**Santa Fe Opera**
PO Box 2408, Santa Fe,
NM 87504-2408, USA

# New York
**Glimmerglass Opera**
PO Box 191, Cooperstown,
NY 13326, USA

**Metropolitan Opera**
Lincoln Center, New York,
NY 10023, USA

**New York City Opera**
20 Lincoln Center, New York,
NY 10023, USA

# North Carolina
**Opera Carolina**
345 N. College Street #409,
Charlotte, NC 28202, USA

# Ohio
**The Cincinnati Opera**
1241 Elm Street, Cincinnati,
OH 45210, USA

**Cleveland Opera**
State Theatre, Playhouse Square
Centre, 1519 Euclid Avenue,
Cleveland, OH 44115-1901, USA

## Pennsylvania
**Opera Company of Philadelphia**
510 Walnut Street, Suite 1500,
Philadelphia, PA 19106, USA

**Pittsburgh Opera**
801 Penn Avenue, Pittsburgh,
PA 15222-3407, USA

## Texas
**Houston Grand Opera**
510 Preston Street, Houston,
TX 77002, USA

**The Dallas Opera**
3102 Oak Lawn Avenue,
Suite 450, Dallas, TX 75219, USA

## Virginia
**The Virginia Opera**
300 W. Franklin Street, Suite 101E,
Richmond, VA 23220, USA

## Washington
**Seattle Opera**
PO Box 9248, Seattle, WA 98109,
USA

# Canadian opera companies

**Calgary Opera**
601, 2378 Avenue SE, Calgary,
AB T2G 5C3, Canada

**The Canadian Opera Co.**
227 Front Street East, Toronto,
Ont M5A 1E8, Canada

**L'Opéra de Montréal**
260 boulevard de Maisonneuve
Ouest, Montréal, QU H2X 1Y9,
Canada

**Vancouver Opera**
Suite 500, 845 Cambie Street,
Vancouver, BC V6B 4Z9, Canada

# Australian and New Zealand opera companies

**The National Opera of Wellington**
Opera House, PO Box 6588,
Wellington, New Zealand

**Opera Australia**
PO Box 291, Strawberry Hill, NSW
2012, Australia

**Opera Queensland**
PO Box 3677, South Brisbane,
Queensland 4101, Australia

**State Opera of South Australia**
PO Box 211, Marlston BC, SA
5033, Australia

**Western Australian Opera**
3rd Floor His Majesty's Theatre, 825
Hay Street, Perth, WA 6000,
Australia

**Auditioning in German-speaking countries**

In many cases, having been taken on to an agent's books within the UK much of your future auditioning will be arranged for you. The cost of travelling very far afield – for instance to America or Australia – must be felt to be wholly justified, provided the sole reason for the journey is to audition.

In contrast, auditioning for the German-speaking companies is a very different matter, and it is worthwhile looking at the system in some detail. The organizational system of 'German' opera houses has been established for years and, like the British Civil Service, is not to be rocked, but understood. The operas are basically scheduled for the years ahead *(der Spielplan)*, and then the singers have to be found to be cast in these operas. Many of these singers will be salaried within their respective *Fächer*. When you audition, the panel will already know the roles that they need to cast, and will be searching for the most useful voices – 'useful' in the sense that a singer can sing as many roles as possible within their *Fach*. The larger opera companies tend to use more guest singers, whereas the smaller companies try to bring them in only to fill the gaps in their casting lists.

After a few years within the system, you may find yourself progressing through different grades of opera houses, although normally you are expected to stay within the same *Fach*. Only the best or biggest voices can make a living by freelancing and/or guesting, and there is a big demand for the heavier voices. When you examine a list of the most-performed operas and operettas in a year in the German opera houses you immediately notice not only the number of Mozart operas performed, but also the 'weighty' pieces, such as *Fidelio*, *Aida*, *Der fliegende Holländer* and *Un ballo in maschera*.

The following is a list of operas and operettas most widely performed within the German system within a typical season:

Over 6,000 performances
    *Die Zauberflöte* (Mozart)

Over 5,000 performances
    *Le nozze di Figaro* (Mozart)

Over 4,500 performances
    *Carmen* (Bizet)
    *La bohème* (Puccini)
    *Zar und Zimmermann* (Lortzing)
    *Madama Butterfly* (Puccini)
    *Il barbiere di Siviglia* (Rossini)
    *Die Entführung aus dem Serail* (Mozart)

Over 4,000 performances
    *Der Freischütz* (Weber)
    *Fidelio* (Beethoven)
    *Rigoletto* (Verdi)
    *Tosca* (Puccini)
    *Il trovatore* (Verdi)

Over 3,500 performances
    *La traviata* (Verdi)
    *Der Wildschütz* (Lortzing)
    *The Bartered Bride* (Smetana)
    *Aida* (Verdi)
    *Les contes d'Hoffmann* (Offenbach)

Over 3,000 performances
    *Così fan tutte* (Mozart)
    *Don Giovanni* (Mozart)
    *I pagliacci* (Leoncavallo)
    *Der fliegende Holländer* (Wagner)
    *Hänsel und Gretel* (Humperdinck)
    *Cavalleria rusticana* (Mascagni)

Over 2,500 performances
    *Un ballo in maschera* (Verdi)
    *Die lustigen Weiber von Windsor* (Nicolai)
    *Der Rosenkavalier* (Strauss)
    *Der Waffenschmied* (Lortzing)

Over 2,000 performances
  *Martha* (Flotow)
  *Otello* (Verdi)
  *Don Pasquale* (Donizetti)
  *La forza del destino* (Verdi)
  *Tannhäuser* (Wagner)
  *Don Carlo* (Verdi)

The requirement in German opera houses for projection and loudness of voice can be greater than elsewhere. This is partly due to the way in which some orchestras play and are conducted, and partly due to the size of some of the houses. For instance, a singer who in the UK usually performs Pamina can find herself cast as Papagena in Germany. Do not be tempted by this demand for heavy voices to push your voice beyond its means – rather strengthen it through development of the speaking voice and the physical strength of the body. Many successful opera singers come from countries with an outdoor life and resonant languages (Sweden and Bulgaria, for example), and often these singers have large bone structures. In many ways, singers are akin to athletes. Singing is really a physical activity requiring absolute strength and fitness, especially for the big roles. After singing a long Wagnerian role, the performer is more likely to be conscious of tired calf muscles, caused by standing for so long on a raked stage, rather than of a tired voice!

**Approaching German opera houses**
Normally you will audition for an opera house through an agent, unless you have a personal connection. In general, German opera companies and agents hold auditions during two periods in the year, and there is usually little point in going at any other time. These two periods can be roughly delineated as September/October and then the following January.

In the first period, the agent will hear you before sending you out to opera houses where there are suitable vacancies. The opera companies will be casting for the contractual year which begins in the following August or September.

The second period for auditions is utilized by the companies to hold re-auditions and further auditions to fill gaps in the casting lists caused either by singers turning down contracts or failure to find suitable singers. Again, the agent will audition you first, unless you are already known to him.

First contact the agents, each of whom covers a specific geographical area. (At the end of this chapter is a list of agents, including the Government agencies.) Let each agent know, in writing, how long you intend to spend in the country, and don't plan too short a stay, since there must be time to send you around to many different opera houses. It is probably better to let your return date remain open. Information about the German opera houses can be found in the *Deutsches Bühnen Jahrbuch* (published annually by Genossenschaft Deutscher Bühner-Angehörigen, Hamburg).

The ability to speak German will be useful and, of course, necessary when you begin work there. The agents and the opera house staff will not usually mind if you cannot speak German at the audition; often they speak fluent English. They will, however, expect you to sing at least one aria in German, and will require good, clear diction. If they offer you a job, they will assume that you will spend the time before taking up your contract learning German. German is an international operatic language in the same way that English is an international business language.

After writing to the agents, you will receive a reply stating the date and time that you are expected for audition (*das Vorsingen*) which you must confirm. When you arrive for your audition, do not be surprised if you discover 20 other singers all waiting to sing at the same time! After seeing the secretary and perhaps fi°lling out an application form (*die Bewerbungsunterlage*), you may find yourself waiting a long time in a cold room, or even outside in the street. Your audition may be long if the agent is interested in your stamina and repertoire. After the audition, the agent may talk to you and/or send you back to the secretary to obtain more details, such as a contact telephone number, so it is best to choose one city as a base for operations, especially a city in the Ruhr district – Düsseldorf, Köln, etc. – where many of the opera houses are clustered in a small area. After this audition, the agent may immediately telephone an opera house, which he knows to have a vacancy suitable for you, and arrange for a further audition there.

Similar circumstances will often arise at an opera house. You arrive at your appointed time of 11 a.m. and find yourself waiting until 4 p.m. On the other hand, you may be offered a contract on the spot.

Remember the rule, mentioned before, that if you choose to sing a certain aria, you are judged on the entire role. It is unlikely that you will have your own pianist with you, so try not to choose a non-repertoire aria for the pianist (*der Korrepetitor*) to play. The audition panel may consist of the opera administrator (*der Intendant*), the musical director (*der Generalmusikdirektor* or *GMD* for short), a conductor (*der Erste/Zweiter Kapellmeister*) and the chorus-master (*der Chorleiter*).

If you are asked whether or not you know a role, be honest for your own good. On one occasion a singer told an agent that she knew the role of Octavian (*Der Rosenkavalier*) and, on the day after she had flown home to London, had a telephone call in the early morning from the agent asking her to fly back immediately to sing Octavian in a performance that night! Naturally, with great embarrassment, she had to confess that she had only *studied* the role, but never performed it. If you are asked about your age, this is the only area where it may pay to be a little vague, for the numerical quantity of this magic figure seems to have much importance attached to it. Opera houses see a singer from a long-term viewpoint, for they hope you may stay some years. Types of contract include normal (two years), one year, guest, single role, and single performance (*Normal-, Jahres-, Gast-, Der Stück- und Abend-Vertrag*).

A singer has a vocal lifetime which an exhausting contract may shorten if care is not taken but, all things considered, to spend a couple of years in a German opera house is very good training. Experiences often include having to learn a major role in five days, and coping with different singers and conductors at various performances. Many times you will walk on stage and see or hear a singer that you have never met before in your life. This happens because performances of one opera are spaced out over the whole season, if not many seasons, so there may be a gap of some months before the next performance. You may learn how to contend with being thrown into a production (*die Regie*) you have never seen, and how to cope with the situations similar to the following: you are playing Rodrigo in *Don Carlo* and, in Act II scene 2, you are directed to walk in a stately manner from the back of the set, through the chorus, down to the front, and to hand a letter to Elisabetta di Valois. As you confidently walk forward, you notice two ladies on either side of the centre, and you realize with horror that you have no idea which is Elisabetta and which is Eboli … One of your roles may be Jochanaan in *Salome*, where a fair amount of the part is sung offstage, as from the cistern, and thus need not be memorized. You arrive in a different town to replace another baritone at short notice, and discover that in their production Jochanaan is chained to a wall in full view of the audience. The afternoon is spent frantically memorizing the offstage passages. Both these incidents actually happened to the same singer.

To sum up the art of auditioning for the German opera houses – remember that you are applying to a business, so use business tactics, be efficient, and keep a cool head.

# Main German and Swiss opera agents

## Government Agencies

**Zentrale Bühnenvermittlung (ZBF) Bonn**
Villemombler Strasse 76,
D-53123 Bonn, Germany
ⓣ +49 228 7130

**ZBF Berlin**
Ordensmeisterstrasse 15, D-12099
Berlin, Germany
ⓣ +49 30 75 7600
ⓕ +49 30 75 760249

**ZBF Leipzig**
Schillerweg 34A, D-04155
Leipzig, Germany
ⓣ +49 341 580 880
ⓕ +49 341 580 8850

## Düsseldorf Area

**Opernagentur Inge Tennigkeit**
Kempener Strasse 4, D-40474
Düsseldorf, Germany

**Reinald Heissler-Remy
Theater Agentur**
Drakestrasse 2, PO Box 110931,
D-40545 Düsseldorf, Germany
ⓣ +49 211 578051
ⓕ +49 211 553498
ⓔ remy.agent@t-online.de

## Frankfurt Area

**Theateragentur Glado von May**
Hermannstrasse 32, D-60318
Frankfurt am Main, Germany
ⓣ +49 692 83347
ⓕ +49 692 95513

**Theateragentur Luisa Petrov**
Glauburgstrasse 95, D-60318
Frankfurt am Main, Germany
ⓣ +49 695 970377
ⓕ +49 695 974808

**Theateragentur Werner Kühnly**
Wörthstrasse 31, D-70563 Stuttgart,
Germany
ⓣ +49 711 780 2764
ⓕ +49 711 780 4403

## Hanover Area

**Theateragentur Hannagret Bueker**

Fuhsestrasse 2, D-30419 Hannover,
Germany

ⓣ +49 511 271 6910

ⓕ +49 511 271 7873

## Munich Area

**Theateragentur Dr Carl F. Jickeli**

Nymphenburgerstrasse 62, D-80335

München, Germany

ⓣ +49 891 239 2626

ⓕ +49 891 239 2627

**Theateragentur Wolfgang Stoll
(Mitarbeiter, Karl-Erich Haase)**

Martiusstrasse 3,
D-80802 München, Germany

ⓣ +49 893 33162

ⓕ +49 893 42674

**Theater und Konzertagentur
Lydia Storle**

Orlandostrasse 8, D-80331
München, Germany

ⓣ +49 892 904766

ⓕ +49 892 904765

**Theater und Konzertagentur
Hermann und Astrid G. Winkler**

Grillparzerstrasse 46, D-81675
München, Germany

ⓣ +49 894 705857

ⓕ +49 894 707123

## Vienna Area

**Künstleragentur Hollaender-Calix**

Grinzinger Allee 46, Haus 2, A-1190
Wien, Austria

ⓣ +43 1 320 5317

ⓕ +43 1 328 4733

**Künstleragentur Dr Raab
und Dr Böhm**

Plankengasse 7, A-1010 Wien,
Austria

ⓣ +43 512 0501

ⓕ +43 512 7743

ⓔ raab.boehm@magnet.at

## Swiss area

**Artists Management Zürich
(Mitarbeiter, Rita Schütz)**

Rütistrasse 52, CH-8044
Zürich-Gockhausen

ⓣ +41 1 821 8957

ⓕ +41 1 821 0127

ⓔ schuetz@artistsman.com

# Other types of audition

**Chorus and choir auditions**

Here the panel is looking for a certain voice to blend into the already established sound of the chorus or choir. The opera chorus panel will be interested in your dramatic possibilities, looks and capability of voice, whereas the choir panel will be more concerned with your sight-reading abilities, intonation, blending and musicality. It is best to prepare for an opera chorus audition as you would prepare for a soloist audition. For a choir audition, prepare a short song and perhaps a difficult modern piece to demonstrate your musical aptitude. In the sight-reading test, keep a cool head and do not be rushed. Try to look at the music as you would at a map, noting the difficult spots. Do not worry if you cannot work them out: at least you will be prepared when they arrive and often they will sort themselves out by instinct. If you panic, you will hurry, so immediately you feel the sensation, do not become even tenser by trying not to panic, but slow yourself down by imagining a kind of sostenuto in the music. Sight-reading aptitude is only gained through practice. The panel may also ask you what your vocal range is and ask you to sing a scale to demonstrate it.

**Radio and recording auditions**

These auditions are concerned with only one thing: the sound quality and communicative power of your voice. Your physical and acting abilities are unimportant, but the microphone's reaction to your voice is vital. The microphone picks up every word, out-of-tune note and distorted sound. It is not interested in your projection or size of voice, only the sound quality.

Some voices are successful in the theatre or the concert hall, but less successful in the studio. It is worth accepting as much recording work as possible, private or commercial, in order to get used to the artificiality of the conditions, and the pressures of 'getting it into the can'.

Often in these auditions there will be no panel present, only the producer and the technician. The BBC used to blank out the window of the control room behind which the panel would sit, but now the producer generally makes a tape to be sent out to the panel and kept on the files. If necessary, you can restart a piece, and this will not be held against you, but the producer will not want to waste precious tape. For radio, after a short balance test, you will normally be expected to launch into a programme of about fifteen minutes, which should be well varied to show off the range of your repertoire. A list of the programme should be prepared, with timings, for the producer, and copies of the music provided. The panel is often interested if you specialize in a certain repertoire, such as Russian song or Baroque music. It will also be interested in your partnership with your pianist, and how good you are as a duo, rather than just as a solo singer.

# Part II
# Recommended Audition Repertoire

# Introduction and voice types

In this section are listed some useful operatic audition arias, standard and not so standard. As explained in the introduction to this book, there are many extant lists of singing repertoire, but few resources available to the opera singer who needs to know just what demands must be met when undertaking a certain aria. Consequently, arias have been arranged chronologically under different voice types, basically corresponding to the German *Fach* system. This is to give a guide to the weight and character of voice expected for an aria, and to give an idea as to which *Fach* a German opera house might feel you belong. A simplified description of each voice type is also included. This provides a sketch of the different attributes. Obviously, any such list is only a general guide, and it may well be that you feel your voice straddles two or more different types. Operatic audition arias for counter-tenors, male altos and male sopranos will, in the main, be gleaned from the Baroque repertoire (mainly Handel, for instance in *Partenope*, Arsace's aria in Act II 'Furibondo spira il vento' in E minor or D minor), with the exception of a few 20th-century pieces, such as Britten's *A Midsummer Night's Dream* (Oberon's 'I know a bank', Act I figure 46) or Reimann's *Lear* (Edgar's scene 'Habe ich mein Leben retten können', Act I scene 4). The vocal demands for this repertoire are very clear, and therefore these voice types are not included in the German *Fach* system, nor have I included such audition pieces in this book.

For each aria, I have given the range of voice needed, timings and a description of the qualities required to sing it. I have also placed the aria in its context within the opera. As far as possible I have kept to the original version of the opera (for example, the Swedish version of Verdi's *Un ballo in maschera),* and to the original language, except where it has become very difficult to find an edition printed in that language. Should this be the case, I have given the original language in the comment.

With arias by Eastern European or Russian composers, it is not generally expected that you should sing in the original language but, at the same time, it would be invidious for me to recommend a good singing translation – this is a matter of personal taste. The transliteration of the Russian titles has been done according to the actual sounding of the Russian words, as opposed to a literal letter-for-letter rendering. The numbering of an aria within an opera is often inconsistent between different editions, but I have tried to give as much information as possible to help track down the aria.

In the comments I have given an idea of the demands an aria may make upon a singer and, if that aria is chosen, what the audition panel might expect to hear. Sometimes I have added a comment for the accompanist, to give him or her some pointers towards the playing of specific arias. If the accompanist is faced with an unknown piece, then the basic harmony, bass and rhythm are the most important aspects of the music to be kept going. In Baroque music especially, the bass is all-important.

Sometimes I have made suggestions of possible cuts to make an aria more concise. In many anthologies the editor has already shortened the arias, but it is useful to know where these cuts take place. For extra cadenzas and alternative coloratura, it is best to refer to Ricci's *Variazioni – Cadenze Tradizioni* published by Ricordi in three volumes. This is referred to as 'Ricci, *Book of Cadenzas*' throughout the rest of this section.

Remember that this is only a selection of arias which I have found to be the most useful. Do not be disappointed to discover your favourite aria is missing – Part III consists of a greatly expanded index of audition arias and timings. I have also included for each voice type (except for the baritone voice) some Handel repertoire, since many opera houses have expanded into Baroque operas.

## Soprano types

### Soubrette

*Qualities*: good language, good middle of voice, as well as top B♭ and C.

*Character*: as the French name suggests – maids, flirtatious young ladies.

*Typical roles*: Despina (*Così fan tutte*), Zerlina (*Don Giovanni*), Susanna (*Le nozze di Figaro*), Marzelline *Fidelio*, Nannetta (*Falstaff*).

### Lyric coloratura (*Lyrischer Koloratur; Koloratur-Soubrette*)

*Qualities*: ability to sing high notes and fast coloratura.

*Character*: very much the same as soubrette.

*Typical roles*: Blonde (*Die Entführung aus dem Serail*), Norma (*Don Pasquale*), Gilda *Rigoletto*, Oscar (*Un ballo in maschera*).

### Lyric (*Lyrischer*)

*Qualities*: ability to sustain long lines; needs more voice than soubrette or lyric coloratura.

*Character*: softer, more sympathetic personality.

*Typical roles*: Pamina (*Die Zauberflöte*), Contessa (*Le nozze di Figaro*), Micaëla (*Carmen*), Lauretta (*Gianni Schicchi*), Mimì (*La bohème*), Liù (*Turandot*).

### Dramatic coloratura

(*Dramatischer Koloratur*)

*Qualities*: ability to sing coloratura with a more powerful and wider range.

*Character*: nobler and more forceful figure.

*Typical roles*: Königen der Nacht (*Die Zauberflöte*), Konstanze (*Die Entführung aus dem Serail*), Fiordiligi (*Così fan tutte*), Lucia (*Lucia di Lammermoor*), Marguerite (*Faust*), Violetta (*La traviata*), Anne Truelove (*The Rake's Progress*).

### Spinto (*Jugendlich-Dramatischer*)

*Qualities*: bigger emotional range and ability to sing long lines in heavier ensembles without tiring.

*Character*: beautiful, central, youthful figure.

*Typical roles*: Agathe (*Der Freischütz*), Elizabeth (*Tannhäuser*), Desdemona (*Otello*), Madama Butterfly, Leonora *Il trovatore*.

### Dramatic *Dramatischer*

*Qualities*: ability to sustain dramatic singing such as is found in Verdi.

*Character*: a woman of strong emotional depths.

*Typical roles*: Fidelio, Aida, Leonora (*La forza del destino*), Amelia (*Un ballo in maschera*), Tosca, Ariadne.

### Heavy dramatic (*Hochdramatischer*)

*Qualities*: ability to sustain long, powerful vocal lines over the orchestra.

*Character*: Goddess-like.

*Typical roles*: Isolde (*Tristan und Isolde*), Senta (*Der fliegende Holländer*), Brünnhilde (*Der Ring des Nibelungen*), Turandot.

## Mezzo-Soprano types

**Lyric** *Lyrischer*; *Spielalt*
*Qualities*: rich middle voice;
flexibility for coloratura.
*Character*: young and able to look
good in 'pants parts'.
*Typical roles*: Cherubino (*Le nozze di
Figaro*), Dorabella (*Così fan tutte*),
Sextus (*La clemenza di Tito*), Rosina
(*Il barbiere di Siviglia*), Cenerentola
(*La Cenerentola*), Siebel (*Faust*).

**Dramatic** (*Dramatischer*)
*Qualities*: greater vocal strength
than a lyric.
*Character*: striking physical
beauty and sustained and dramatic
authority on stage.
*Typical roles*: Leonora (*La favorita*),
Carmen, Dalila (*Samson et Dalila*),
Charlotte (*Werther*), Eboli (*Don
Carlo*).

**Contralto**
(*Dramatischer Alt; Tiefer Alt*)
*Qualities*: mature voice with stronger
lower range and heavier colour.
*Character*: same as dramatic.
*Typical roles*: Azucena (*Il trovatore*),
Ulrica (*Un ballo in maschera*), Erda
(*Der Ring des Nibelungen*), Gäa
(*Daphne*).

## Tenor types

**Buffo** (*Spieltenor*)
*Qualities*: flexibility of voice
and good diction.
*Character*: good actor, ability to suc-
ceed in *comprimario* parts (secondary
roles).

*Typical roles*: Pedrillo (*Die
Entführung aus dem Serail*),
Vašek (*The Bartered Bride*),
Beppe (*I pagliacci*).

**Lyric** (*Lyrischer*)
*Qualities*: similar to the buffo,
but also an ability to sing Mozart.
*Character*: handsome, youthful
figure.
*Typical roles*: Don Ottavio
(*Don Giovanni*), Tamino (*Die
Zauberflöte*), Alfredo (*La traviata*),
Werther, Tom Rakewell
(*The Rake's Progress*).

**Italian** (*Italienischer*)
*Qualities*: more robust voice
than a lyric with a good high C.
*Character*: strong and romantic.
*Typical roles*: Edgardo (*Lucia di
Lammermoor*), Faust, Rodolfo (*La
bohème*), Il Duca (*Rigoletto*).

**Youthful heroic**
(*Jugendlicher Heldentenor*)
*Qualities*: voice of great ringing qual-
ity, a good top and staying power.
*Character*: young and commanding.
*Typical roles*: Don José (*Carmen*),
Max (*Der Freischütz*), Cavaradossi
(*Tosca*), Calaf (*Turandot*).

**Heroic** (*Heldentenor*)
*Qualities*: strong voice able
to carry over the orchestra
with impact.
*Character*: hero-like.
*Typical roles*: Florestan (*Fidelio*),
Otello, Siegmund (*Die Walküre*),
Tannhäuser.

## Baritone types

**Lyric** (*Lyrischer, Spielbariton*)
*Qualities*: flexible voice throughout range up to G; ability to sing Mozart.
*Character*: good actor.
*Typical roles*: Papageno (*Die Zauberflöte*), Figaro (*Il barbiere di Siviglia*), Malatesta (*Don Pasquale*).

**Cavalier** (*Kavalier*)
*Qualities*: heavier voice than a lyric.
*Character*: attractive and strong stage presence.
*Typical roles*: Il Conte (*Le nozze di Figaro*), Don Giovanni, Valentine (*Faust*), Eugene Onegin, Germont (*La traviata*).

**Character** (*Charakter*)
*Qualities*: powerful voice with ringing high register; ability to sing Verdi and Puccini.
*Character*: ability to command the stage.
*Typical roles*: Escamillo (*Carmen*), Rigoletto, Renato (*Un ballo in maschera*), Tonio (*I pagliacci*).

**Heroic** (*Heldenbariton, Hoher Bass*)
*Qualities*: big voice; ability to sound cruel and to be able to sing heavy Verdi.
*Character*: ability to portray power.
*Typical roles*: Pizarro (*Fidelio*), Amfortas (*Parsifal*), Macbeth.

## Bass types

**Buffo** (*Spielbass*)
*Qualities*: flexible voice, with a wide range of expression.
*Character*: excellent actor capable of many and varied roles.
*Typical roles*: Leporello (*Don Giovanni*), Bartolo (*Il barbiere di Siviglia*), Osmin (*Die Entführung aus dem Serail*).

**Bass-baritone**
(*Charakterbass*; *Basso cantante*)
*Qualities*: darker and slightly more dramatic quality of voice than a buffo.
*Character*: the same as the buffo.
*Typical roles*: Figaro (*Le nozze di Figaro*), Basilio (*Il barbiere di Siviglia*), Méphistophélès (*Faust*).

**Basso-profondo** (*Seriöser Bass*)
*Qualities*: deep voice with rich quality.
*Character*: imposing figure with intelligence and sensitivity, inspiring confidence.
*Typical roles*: Sarastro (*Die Zauberflöte*), Filippo (*Don Carlo*), Gremin (*Eugene Onegin*), Fiesco (*Simon Boccanegra*).

# French Operatic Arias
## *for Soprano*

### EP7552 £14.95

| | | |
|---|---|---|
| Auber | Quel bonheur, je respire | Fra Diavolo |
| Berlioz | Entre l'amour | Benvenuto Cellini |
| Bizet | Comme autrefois | Les pêcheurs de perles |
| Delibes | Où va la jeune Indoue | Lakmé |
| Gounod | Ah ! Je ris de me voir | Faust |
| Gounod | Il était un roi | Faust |
| Gounod | Ô légère hirondelle | Mireille |
| Gounod | Je veux vivre | Roméo et Juliette |
| Lalo | Lorsque je t'ai vu | Le roi d'Ys |
| Massenet | Pleurez, mes yeux ! | Le Cid |
| Massenet | Obéissons | Manon |
| Massenet | Adieu, notre petite table | Manon |
| Massenet | Dis-moi que je suis belle | Thaïs |
| Meyerbeer | Parmi les pleurs | Les Huguenots |
| Offenbach | Les oiseaux dans la charmille | Les contes d'Hoffmann |
| Offenbach | Elle a fui | Les contes d'Hoffmann |
| Rossini | Sombre forêt | Guillaume Tell |
| Thomas | Je suis Titania | Mignon |
| Verdi | Toi qui sus le néant | Don Carlos |

# Soprano arias

## Soubrette soprano

1. **Deh vieni, non tardar** (Susanna)
   (Recit: Giunse alfin il momento)
   Le nozze di Figaro (1786), Act IV no 27
   Mozart [3'30"]  📖 EP734, EP4231A

*Near Seville, 18th century: Susanna, who is dressed as the Countess (as arranged by Figaro), is out in the garden at night. She knows that Figaro is secretly watching her, and plays on his jealousy by pretending to be waiting for the Count. She hints that she will follow her instincts and will respond to the rapturous atmosphere of the garden by letting love take her over.*

This aria has a deceptively wide range and needs beautiful tone and line throughout. The recitative requires much atmospheric colour; the amoral text needs to be fully brought out and any added appoggiaturas should not interfere with the flow and charm of the text and music. The aria is in the 'serenade' mode, normally reserved for men, therefore the line needs to imitate that kind of sexual urge – quite a radical statement for that period. The caesura marks near the end of the aria denote possible places for tasteful cadenzas.

**2. Batti, batti, o bel Masetto** (Zerlina)
(Recit: Ma se colpo io non ho)
Don Giovanni (1787), Act I no 13
Mozart [4'20"]   EP734, EP4231A

*Seville, 17th century: Masetto is understandably annoyed that his bride-to-be, Zerlina, has been taken away by Don Giovanni on Masetto's wedding day. When she returns, in order to pacify Masetto's suspicions about her, Zerlina invites him to beat her; she can then kiss the hands that have hurt her, and peace will be restored.*

A useful aria containing first a slow and then a more dancing section (it is best to begin with the end of the secco recitative). It needs a light, unobtrusive top to the voice, and much charm and femininity. The pianist must be continually aware of the cello obbligato semiquaver part, which unites the tempo and music of the two sections. In the second section, the dotted crotchet pulse ideally should match the crotchet pulse of the first section. The text in some versions gives 'contento' instead of 'contenti', and the text underlay in the last four bars of the voice part is as follows: vo-'gliam' (on the first beat), 'pas-' (second beat), '-sar' (first beat) in both phrases.

**3. In uomini, in soldati** (Despina)
Così fan tutte (1790), Act I no 12
Mozart [2'25"]   EP4474

*Naples, 18th century: Despina, a maid, asks Fiordiligi and Dorabella if they can give an example of a man (or soldier) who is faithful. She tells them not to trust men, and to fool them in the same way that men fool women.*

A light and dancing aria needing good diction. The words should be full of cynicism. The trills of 'la ra la' must be cleanly executed and variety of phrasing is extremely important throughout. Remember that the repetition of the text possibly derives from the fact that you are singing to two naïve girls who come from northern Italy and know nothing about real Neapolitan life. The caesuras are opportunities for small, tasteful cadenzas.

**4. Una donna a quindici anni** (Despina)
Così fan tutte (1790), Act II no 19
Mozart [3'15"] 📖 EP734, EP4231A

*Naples, 18th century: Despina tells Fiordiligi and Dorabella how every girl should know the art of attracting a man, even from the age of 15 years.*

This needs more line than Despina's first aria and, like Zerlina's music (*Don Giovanni*), requires much fluidity of voice. All the ornaments should be sung on the beat, and the false ending should be communicated with great humour. Mozart's music is purposefully childlike, so ensure that the text is correctly phrased. Important words are often set off the beat, e.g. 'par ch'ab<u>bian</u> <u>gu</u>sto di tal dot<u>tri</u>na, <u>vi</u>va Des<u>pi</u>na che <u>sa</u> ser<u>vir</u>.'

**5. O wär ich schon mit dir vereint** (Marzelline)
Fidelio (1805), Act I no 2
Beethoven [4'] 📖 EP734, EP4231A

*Seville, 18th century: Jacquino, who loves Marzelline, has just left her on stage alone. She muses on her own secret love for Fidelio, and her desire to be able to confess this love to him. In the second verse, she pictures the domestic bliss in which they could live.*

The aria's range can make it hard to sound interesting. It has two verses, and needs good diction and phrasing. In each verse there should be a strong contrast between the clear declamatory style and the Italianate outburst of feeling that follows. It is best only to go up to an F in the final complete bar of singing.

**6. Sul fil d'un soffio etesio** (Nannetta)
Falstaff (1893), Act III sc 2 fig 35
Verdi [4'15"]

*Windsor Great Park, c.1400: As part of the masquerade to frighten Falstaff by Herne's Oak, Nannetta and the children are dressed as fairies. She invokes in magical language the fairy dance which follows. In the second verse she sings of the magical power which lies hidden in the perfume of the flowers which they pick.*

This requires a silvery line and a wonderful legato, as smooth as glass. Include the final phrase after the second chorus which goes up to the held top A. You can begin the aria at 'Ninfe! Elfi!' (figure 33), and then, after 'Ombre serene!', cut to 'Sul fil d'un soffio etesio' (figure 35). The pianist must play very delicately and create a very transparent texture, not allowing any weight of tone to intrude.

7. **Quando me'n vo'** (Musetta)
   La bohème (1896), Act II fig 21
   Puccini [2'25"] 📖 EP9637

*Paris, 1830: Musetta, Marcello's old flame, sings this taunting aria behind his back while her 'sugar-daddy' Alcindoro tries to stop her from causing a scene. She tells how everyone stops to look at her when she walks in the street, and all their secret desires become apparent. She knows how much Marcello is struggling with his desire for her.*

A short aria requiring stylish use of rubato, good lower range and clear top. The waltz feeling must never be lost, and the legato phrases, always marked by Puccini with a slur, must be well delivered. It is helpful if the pianist makes Mimì's part very clear in the second half.

8. **Depuis le jour** (Louise)
   Louise (1900), Act III sc 1
   Charpentier [4']

*Paris, 1900: Louise is a working girl in love with an artist named Julien although her parents are unhappy with the relationship. She sings to Julien of her happiness, remembering her first kiss.*

The fluid phrases of this aria need skill in floating the voice, using a delicious silver-like beauty of tone. The accompaniment should be very fluid in tempo to allow expressive rubato in the vocal part.

9. **Non, monsieur, mon mari** (Thérèse)
   Les mamelles de Tirésias (1947), Act I fig 20
   Poulenc [5'15"]

*French Riviera, 1910: In an imaginary town on the French Riviera,
Thérèse decides to go on strike and become a man. She would prefer to have
a masculine career like a soldier rather than do as her husband pleases (he
shouts at her from offstage to bring him some lard). At this point she releases her balloon breasts, one red, one blue, and then, in the waltz music,
laughingly tells how vice is after all a dangerous thing to practise. It is better to be virtuous. She sacrifices her symbols of femininity by exploding
them with a lighted match, puts on a false beard, and sets out (in a
Spanish dance) to fight against her husband.*

A fast, flashy aria, which is full of declamatory text, high C's, and two
sexy dances. It demands an uninhibited character to sing this piece. For
the pianist, this is an exhilarating piece to play, demanding great use of
the sustaining pedal (as is the case with most of Poulenc's piano music).

# Lyric coloratura soprano

**10. Piangerò la sorte mia** (Cleopatra)
(Recit: E pur così in un giorno)
Giulio Cesare (1724), Act III sc 3 no 32
Handel [5'15"]

*Egypt, AD 48: After being defeated by Caesar at the battle of Pharsalus,
Pompeo found refuge with Tolomeo (Ptolomy, King of Egypt), only to be
assassinated by Achilla, the captain of the guard. Pompeo's son, Sesto,
having sworn revenge, has been imprisoned, and Pompeo's wife, Cornelia,
bas been sent to a harem. Cleopatra, Tolomeo's sister, sings this lament
in prison. She was trying to seduce Caesar when Tolomeo's soldiers arrived
in an attempt to kill him, an attempt foiled by Caesar's leaping into
the sea. In the middle section, she imagines she will return as a ghost to
haunt her brother.*

Secco recitative followed by an aria with a slow legato line and a fast,
brilliant middle section. The da capo section can be tastefully ornamented. The original key is E major. The lament was an important
technique of mourning to ease the mind of its grief. The aria's outer
sections must be treated as a formal shape through which Cleopatra's

emotions are released. Only in the middle section should her sup-
pressed desire for revenge be demonstrated without inhibition. The
recitative is a clear summing-up of the disasters which have befallen
her; time should be allowed for each detail to make its mark. The
panel will be looking for clarity of thought and disciplined use of
colour in the voice.

**11. Tornami a vagheggiar** (Morgana)
   Alcina (1735), Act I (end)
   Handel [5']

*An Enchanted Island: Morgana is sister to Alcina, an enchantress who lives
on an island enticing lovers, who are then transformed into different forms
of life. Alcina's latest captive is a knight named Ruggiero, but a new rival
has appeared in the shape of Bradamante (Ruggiero's former lover), who
has disguised herself as her brother Ricciardo. Morgana is infatuated with
Ricciardo, and urges 'him' to flee.*

A useful da capo aria as it is not too long. It requires a good floated
high B♭ and good agility. The final words in the middle section are
'cara mia spene', 'spene' is an old poetical form of 'speme' given in
order to rhyme with the end of the A section 'mio bene'.

**12. Padre, germani, addio!** (Ilia)
   (Recit: Quanti mi siete intorno)
   Idomeneo (1781), Act I no 1
   Mozart [4'10"]  📖 EP1127

*Crete, after the Trojan wars: Ilia, a Trojan princess, has been taken as
prisoner to Crete where she has fallen in love with the King's son,
Idamante. She describes her hatred for her captors, which is outweighed
by her love for Idamante.*

Begin with the end of the accompanied recitative in order to demonstrate the dramatic change into the beginning of the aria, which
demands clean, fluid singing and wonderful phrasing. The runs must
be perfectly shaped.

**13. Zeffiretti lusinghieri** (Ilia)
(Recit: Solitudini amiche)
Idomeneo (1781), Act III no 16 or 19
Mozart [6']  📖 EP4231A

*Crete, after the Trojan Wars: Ilia, a Trojan princess, sent as prisoner to
Crete, expresses her love for the King's son, Idamante.*

Requires fluid singing, clear runs, good intonation and understanding
of the harmonies underneath the sustained notes. The triplets in the
accompaniment should be illustrative of the zephyr wind.

**14. Durch Zärtlichkeit and Schmeicheln** (Blonde)
Die Entführung aus dem Serail (1782), Act II no 8
Mozart [3' cut version]  📖 EP4231A

*Turkey, 16th century: Blonde tells Osmin off for ordering her around. She
is a European girl who must be encouraged to work with tenderness and
kindness, not by cajoling.*

Beautiful phrases with some high climbing melismas, where you should
allow space for the top C♯ in order to prepare for the top E's. The contrast between the tender music and the cajoling music must be clearly
defined. The Bärenreiter edition offers the aria in full, though it is
better to audition with the standard cut version.

**15. Quel bonheur, je respire** (Zerline)
(Recit: Ne craignez rien, Milord)
Fra Diavolo (1830), Act II no 7
Auber [3'30"]  📖 EP7552

*Near Naples, 18th century: Zerline is tidying a room in an inn ready for
the English Lord Kookburn who is travelling to Italy. She is looking forward to being free to spend time with her secret love Lorenzo, an officer in
the Dragoons.*

A short recitative followed by a charming aria with showy cadenzas.
There is a danger of the aria becoming rather four-square, so let the
phrasing of the melody communicate lots of charm.

### 16. **O luce di quest'anima** (Linda)

(Recit: Ah! tardai troppo)

Linda di Chamounix (1842), Act I no 4

Donizetti [4'30"] (originally in D♭, up a semitone)

📖 EP2074

*Chamounix (Savoy), 1760: Linda is the daughter of Antonio, who leases a farm from the Marchese de Boisfleury and owes him money. Linda has gone to meet her lover, a painter called Carlo, and has just missed him. She finds some flowers left by him and sings how she adores him in spite of their poverty.*

This is a bravura coloratura aria with a wide range and use of declamation. See Ricci, *Book of Cadenzas* for alternative ornamentation. The pianist must be prepared for all the stringendos and calandos in the accompaniment.

### 17. **Quel guardo il cavaliere** (Norina)

Don Pasquale (1843), Act I sc 2 no 4

Donizetti [5'45"] 📖 EP4231B

*Rome, early-19th century: Norina reads from a chivalrous romance and laughs at the sentiments within it. She knows the power of a glance but also all the other ploys girls utilize to control men.*

Norina has to demonstrate a wide range of mood and the aria demands much naughtiness and sparkle. Donizetti often writes with humour in this opera, which seems almost a pastiche of his earlier, more serious operas. The coloratura must illustrate the text and the acciaccaturas must not be sung off the voice; the differences in the melody when the text 'Ho testa bizarra' is sung for the second time should be fully communicated. The cavatina can also show off the singer's legato. In the full score, under the sixth bar of singing, the bass moves to C♯ in the middle of the bar. In the second verse of the fast section, a cut can be made to the second occurrence of 'D'un breve sorrisetto'. The first four vocal notes of the Poco più should be B♭'s. This section can be cut, but it does contain a wonderful demonstration of a singing exercise. (See Ricci, *Book of Cadenzas*.)

**18. Wohl denn! gefasst ist der Entschluss** (Anna Reich)
Die lustigen Weiber von Windsor (1849), Act III no 11
Nicolai [5'30" cut and short intro.] 📖 EP734, EP4231B

*Windsor, c.1400: Mrs Page dresses Anne for the masquerade to trick
Falstaff. Although Mrs Page wants her to wear red so that Cajus can recognize her, and though Mr Page wishes her to wear green so that Slender can
spot her, Anne tricks both these would-be husbands, and her parents. She
sends the green robe to Cajus and the red to Slender, so that they will be
'united' while she, dressed in white like the fairy queen Titania, will claim
her true love, Fenton. She sings of her happiness and love.*

This aria is dangerously long for audition purposes, containing recitative, cavatina and cabaletta, but it can be cut from the end of the 20th
bar of the Allegro vivace to the 58th bar, and also from the end of the
75th bar to the 86th bar, changing the text in bar 75 to 'vor meinem'.
It is very wide ranging, and contains some very difficult climbing passages up to high B. It needs good flexibility and a beautifully sung line.

**19. Caro nome** (Gilda)
(Recit: Gualtier Maldè!)
Rigoletto (1851), Act I sc 2
Verdi [4'45"] 📖 EP4246A

*Mantua, 16th century: Gilda, daughter of the court jester, Rigoletto, has
been followed by a student who has confessed his love for her. She admits
her own love for him, not knowing that he is really the Duke of Mantua.
He, in turn, does not know that she is the jester's daughter. Disturbed by a
noise in the street he escapes, but not before telling her that his name is
Gualtier Maldè. In this aria she describes the feelings this name invokes,
and how her last sigh would be always for him.*

A difficult coloratura aria, requiring wide range and clear fluid runs.
Cadenzas should be chosen with care (see Ricci, *Book of Cadenzas*), and
it is best to end with the long cadenza and not continue to the ending
with the chorus. The portamentos between the phrases must be executed beautifully, and the underlay of text in the long melismas can be
altered if necessary. The pianist should be fully aware of the possible
tenutos in the voice part.

**20. Volta la terrea** (Oscar)
Un ballo in maschera (1859), Act I sc 1 fig 21
Verdi [1'45"] 📖 EP4246B

*Sweden, 1792: A judge has appeared before Gustavus III (Riccardo) accusing a negress, Mme Arvidson (Ulrica), of criminal activity. Oscar, the King's page, asks permission to defend her, saying that she is only a clever fortune-teller and, laughingly, that she must be in league with the devil because she is so successful.*

A light, two-verse aria showing off staccato singing and clear runs. It requires good intonation.

**21. Saper vorreste** (Oscar)
Un ballo in maschera (1859), Act III sc 2 fig 53
Verdi [1'50"] 📖 EP4246B

*Sweden, 1792: At the masked ball, Anckarstroem (Renato) is searching for King Gustavus (Riccardo) in order to kill him, but does not know his disguise. He recognizes the page, Oscar, and interrogates him about the King's dress. In this aria, Oscar teases him that he knows the answer, but his beating heart will keep it a secret.*

A short, two-verse arietta that demonstrates both staccato and legato singing. Make it very clear whether you are singing over the pauses without a breath, or taking one.

**22. Je suis Titania (Polonaise)** (Philene)
(Recit: Ah! pour ce soir)
Mignon (1866), Act II sc 2 no 12C
Thomas [5'] 📖 EP7552

*Germany, late-18th century: Philene, an actress, flushed with success from her performance in* A Midsummer Night's Dream, *sings this aria – 'I am Titania and make all happy. All night my elves provide my light and at dawn you find me roaming over land and sea.'*

This is a tour de force of coloratura singing, ideally needing a top E♭. As it stands, it is too long for audition purposes, but it can be cut from the third beat of bar 42 to the upbeat to the fourth bar after the key change back to B♭ major. There should be much variety in the grouping and phrasing of the coloratura and little weight on the barlines, except where marked. The pianist must accompany with due understanding of the shape of the vocal line.

**23. Je veux vivre (Waltz)** (Juliette)
Roméo et Juliette (1867), Act I no 3
Gounod [3'15"] 📖 EP7552

*Verona, 14th century: Juliet is with her nurse resting from the excitement of the Capulets' ball. Juliet interrupts the nurse's comment that she was already married at Juliet's age by telling her enthusiastically how she prefers to remain in the spring of life, which is her youth.*

A light aria requiring flexibility and style. The original key is F major. The acciaccaturas should be accurately sung and the melody phrased in long 'bows'. Imagine that the accompaniment is the dance music resounding from the ballroom.

**24. Spiel'ich die Unschuld vom Lande –**
   **Audition aria** (Adele)
Die Fledermaus (1874), Act III no 14
Johann Strauss [4'30"] 📖 EP9777

*Vienna, late-19th century: Adele, a maid, and her sister Ida have met Frank, a prison governor, at a party given by Russian Prince Orlofsky. They arrive at the prison the next morning to ask if Frank would help Adele in her stage career. She sings this aria to demonstrate her talent, by first characterizing a village flirt, then a queen and finally an aristocratic lady from Paris who is having an affair with a young Count.*

A bright coloratura aria, full of character changes, needing a good sense of humour and delivery. The passages with no text (i.e. the melismas set to 'la' or 'ah') should be full of meaning and innuendo and avoid the impression that the singer has forgotten the words. The pianist must not rush in the final section in order to give the singer plenty of time to act out the story, especially during the suggestive 'ah's'.

**25. Les oiseaux dans la charmille – Doll's Song** (Olympia)
Les contes d'Hoffmann (1881), Act I no 9A or 12
Offenbach [5'20"] 📖 EP7552

*Munich, 19th century: Olympia, a pretend daughter of Spalanzani, is really an automated doll. She performs this song to the assembled guests, proclaiming that everything sings of love for a young girl. During both verses she winds down at the end of the cadenza and has to be wound up by Spalanzani.*

This is a virtuoso coloratura aria which shows off technique but not much else. The second verse can be ornamented. The 'winding down' can often sound embarrassing in an audition; therefore it is best omitted and sung as written. The pianist must always allow time for the singer's breaths.

**26. Où va la jeune Hindoue – Scène et**
**légende de la fille du Paria** (Lakmé)
Lakmé (1883), Act II no 10
Delibes [6'45"] 📖 EP7552

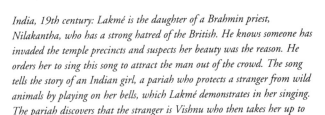

*India, 19th century: Lakmé is the daughter of a Brahmin priest, Nilakantha, who has a strong hatred of the British. He knows someone has invaded the temple precincts and suspects her beauty was the reason. He orders her to sing this song to attract the man out of the crowd. The song tells the story of an Indian girl, a pariah who protects a stranger from wild animals by playing on her bells, which Lakmé demonstrates in her singing. The pariah discovers that the stranger is Vishnu who then takes her up to heaven, leaving the sound of bells still ringing.*

This beautiful high coloratura aria, known as the Bell Song, requires silvery tone, elegant singing and a good ability for story-telling. Make a cut from the end of the opening cadenza to the Andante.

**27. Adieu, notre petite table** (Manon)
(Recit: Allons! Il le faut)
Manon (1884), Act II fig 123
Massenet [3'15"] 📖 EP7552

*Paris 1721: Manon, a young girl on her way to a convent, has met Des Grieux and they are now living together in Paris. Lescaut, her cousin, and Brétigny, a neighbour in love with Manon, noisily arrive. Lescaut asks Des Grieux if he proposes to marry Manon. While Des Grieux shows Lescaut a letter that he has just written to his father, proposing exactly that, Brétigny quietly warns Manon that Des Grieux's father is planning to kidnap his son and thus the way could now be open for their own love affair. Lescaut and Brétigny leave, followed shortly by Des Grieux, who goes to post the letter to his father. Manon, alone, starts to have doubts about her love for Des Grieux and finds herself singing the passionate music that Brétigny had sung earlier (Andante espressivo). She sings a fond farewell to her little table where they spent many hours sitting, happy in their love.*

A dramatic recitative needing big singing, followed by an arioso needing tenderness and fragility of tone. Here the range is quite low. The dynamics both in the voice and the accompaniment should be strictly observed and a feeling of spontaneity engendered, without any hint of sentimentality or sadness.

### 28. Je marche sur tous les chemins
**(Gavotte)** (Manon)
Manon (1884), Act III fig 189
Massenet [5'15"]

*Paris, 1721: Manon is now with her new lover, Brétigny, after Des Grieux was kidnapped by his father's servants. The holiday crowd is making merry on the* Cours la Reine; *Manon arrives in a sedan chair and sings a song to them in praise of youth and pleasure. She is like a queen with no rivals and, if she dies, may she die in laughter. Let us always obey love and enjoy ourselves.*

This is a very extrovert aria and a really good show piece. The recitative followed by a two-verse gavotte requires a good middle voice and a wonderful coloratura top. The accompaniment should conjure up the feeling of the crowd surrounding Manon, reacting to and applauding her words.

**29. Stridono lassù (Ballatella)** (Nedda)
(Recit: Qual fiamma avea nel guardo)
I pagliacci (1892), Act I fig 36
Leoncavallo [4'40"]

*Calabria, 1865–70: Nedda has noticed the fierce, searching look of her husband, Canio, and wonders if her secret love-affair has been discovered. She cheers herself up by enjoying the sun and the birds, and sings of the freedom and joy that bird life communicates.*

The line lies in the middle of the voice and this needs rich but flexible singing. This aria requires good phrasing against a rhythmical accompaniment. The orchestral accompaniment in the Vivace is very sustained.

**30. Glitter and be gay** (Cunegonde)
Candide (1956), Act I no 7
Bernstein [3'45" cut]

*Lisbon, legendary: Cunegonde, the baron's virgin daughter, fell in love with Candide, a bastard cousin. He was exiled when they were discovered together. Since then the family has been massacred by soldiers while Cunegonde wanders from brothel to brothel. She sings of how she must always appear happy and yet, in spite of everything, she does enjoy all the luxuries which surround her.*

A brilliant, high coloratura aria, which is extremely difficult. It consists of a slow, languid waltz followed by a fast dance, some dialogue over the waltz, and the dance again but extended. This aria is rather long and it would be better to cut from the end of the first Allegretto molto section (omit the last five bars) to the coda section (Un poco più mosso).

**31. Come, now a roundel** (Tytania)
A Midsummer Night's Dream (1960), Act I fig 94
Britten [2'5"]

*A wood near Athens, legendary: Tytania enters with her fairies and asks for a lullaby to send her to sleep.*

A short, soft coloratura aria in which it is hard to sustain the tessitura and keep in tune, especially on the recurring F#'s and in the descending phrase in the third bar before the end. The pianist should begin six bars before figure 94 and make sure that the F#'s (on the glockenspiel) are always clear.

# Lyric soprano

**32. Porgi amor** (Contessa)
Le nozze di Figaro (1786), Act II no 10
Mozart [2'10" with shortened intro.]

EP4231A, EP734, EP8901,

*Near Seville, 18th century: The Countess prays to the god of love to restore her husband's love for her.*

A short aria requiring utmost repose and line of voice. It should only be attempted if you are in total control and can produce a feeling of aristocratic purity. Shape the melisma semiquavers as beautifully as possible – these gorgeous lines prove that the Countess truly loves her husband.

**33. Dove sono** (Contessa)
(Recit: E Susanna non vien!)
Le nozze di Figaro (1786), Act III no 19
Mozart [5'30"]    EP4231A, EP734, EP8901

*Near Seville, 18th century: The Countess is anxiously awaiting Susanna's return. Susanna is with the Count persuading him to meet her in the garden that night where she and the Countess will switch clothes to trick him. The Countess muses on her unhappy state reduced to playing these games. In the aria she remembers the happy days of love; can she hope that her constant devotion to her husband will reap its just reward?*

A recitative full of colour changes, followed by an aria with long melodic line needing special control of the breath, especially in the repeat where the phrases are joined together in four-bar groups. Be careful that the last line of the recitative does not lose tension, in order that the new nostalgic tone of the aria is apparent. Great care should be taken with the intonation of the phrase 'Perchè mai, se in pianti e in pene' when it turns from major to minor. The Allegro needs good pacing and a fine top to the voice, but still with good line.

**34. Mi tradì quell'alma ingrata** (Donna Elvira)
(Recit: In quali eccessi)
Don Giovanni (Vienna 1788), Act II no 23
Mozart [5'30"] EP8901

*Seville, 17th century: Donna Elvira is troubled by two opposing emotions: the knowledge that heaven has to punish Don Giovanni, and the fact that she still loves him and wishes to save him.*

The tessitura lies around top F and G and demands good control, beautiful line and fluid runs. The recitative requires strong colours in the voice. In the full score, in the long melisma on 'palpitando' there is a Db at the fourth quaver of the second bar and a D♮ at the fourth quaver of the third bar. In spite of the strength of the text, the vocal and orchestral music must be allowed to flow as if Elvira's love for Don Giovanni can never be shaken.

**35. Non più di fiori vaghe catene** (Vitellia)
La clemenza di Tito (1791), Act II sc 2 no 23
Mozart [6'45"] EP794, EP4231A

*Rome, AD 79–81: Vitellia, who trapped Sesto into organizing a conspiracy against the Roman Emperor's life, hears of Sesto's imminent execution and decides to confess her involvement. She faces up to her destiny and sings that whoever saw her suffering would have pity on her.*

This aria lies very low in parts and, if you have very good low notes, it is worth singing. Many of the pauses need to be filled out with cadenzas as was the practice of the day. After the first 62 bars of the Allegro, a cut may be made from the pause to the upbeat into bar 100.

**36. Ach, ich fühl's** (Pamina)
Die Zauberflöte (1791), Act II no 17
Mozart [3'30"] 📖 EP734, EP4231A

*Egypt, legendary: Pamina finds Tamino in Sarastro's temple but does not know he is under a vow of silence. She takes his silence as heartlessness and tries to make him respond, even as far as threatening suicide.*

This aria requires a perfect line and fluid runs, over a sparse accompaniment. Each phrase is markedly different and the intonation of the chromatic notes is extremely important. The silences between the phrases must be full of tension, to convey that Pamina is for ever hoping that Tamino will answer her. A difficult piece to sing out of context, but if successfully brought off, worth doing.

**37. Oh! quante volte** (Giulietta)
(Recit: Eccomi in lieta vesta)
I Capuleti e i Montecchi (1839), Act I sc 4
Bellini [5'45"]

*Verona, 13th century: Juliet of the Capulet family has been forcibly betrothed to Tebaldo, though she loves Romeo of the Montagues, the rival family. She is in her room, dressed in bridal clothes, and feels that she is like a sacrificial victim at Hymen's altar; if only Hymen's torch would burn and consume her. 'Where art thou, Romeo? How often I have prayed for you, but all is in vain.'*

This is a beautiful aria with a lyrical recitative, which shows off cantabile, soft singing. In the full score at the word 'Romeo' in the recitative, the last note is B♭. Make sure that you sing a C♮ after the turn, in the bars containing the text 'con quale l'ardor'. The underlay at the end of the first verse in the full score has the second syllable of 'mio' on the top G, F and E♭, and the final four notes of the phrase are sung to the text 'il mio desir!' The pianist should cut the introductory six bars of the Andante sostenuto.

**38. Comme autrefois dans la nuit sombre** (Leïla)

(Recit: Me voilà seule dans la nuit)

Les pêcheurs de perles (1863), Act II no 7

Bizet [5'] 📖 EP7552

*Ceylon, antiquity: Leïla, a Brahmin priestess, is secretly in love with Nadir, a fisherman. She is warned by the High Priest to stay faithful to her vows. Overlooking the sea, she waits for her lover and imagines him waiting for her and that he will keep her safe.*

A short recitative is followed by an aria with sweeping phrases.
The cadenza can be shortened by leaving out the melisma on 'Ah!'.
The panel will expect mellifluous phrasing, with the high notes fully integrated into the line. The accompaniment should also be very fluid and legato.

**39. Je dis que rien ne m'épouvante** (Micaëla)

Carmen (1875), Act III no 22

Bizet [4'30"]

*Seville, 1820: Micaëla has fearfully climbed the hill where a band of smugglers have their hide-out. She has come to rescue Don José from the clutches of Carmen, for the sake of his mother. She turns to God, praying that He will protect her from fear.*

An emotional aria demanding a rich middle voice and a marvellous top for the music's great, sweeping phrases. The recitative is by Guiraud, so it is best to omit it. Notice that the rhythm for 'dont les artifices maudits' should be equal quavers. Normally the phrase 'Seigneur, vous me protégerez!' is sung after the chord finishes in the orchestra; it is marked *colla voce*. The panel will expect a magical transition back to the original music and a long *messa di voce* on the penultimate note of the aria.

**40. Ebben? ... Ne andrò lontana** (La Wally)

La Wally (1892), Act I letter PP

Catalani [3'30"]

*Tyrol, 1800: On the 70th birthday of Stromminger, Giuseppe Hagenbach tells of his exploits. Stromminger provokes a quarrel because he recognizes Hagenbach as the son of an old rival, but La Wally, Stromminger's daughter, intervenes and says she loves him. Stromminger tells her either to marry Gellner, who loves her, or to leave the house. She says how sad it is to leave, perhaps never to return.*

A slow sustained aria needing an intensity of line and a wonderful high B near the end. The lower notes need careful phrasing so that they are fully integrated into the line. In the sixth bar of singing, the second syllable of 'bianca' should come on the second beat on a repeated E and then, using the marked portamento, reach the B on the third beat.

### 41. Sì. Mi chiamono Mimì (Mimì)
La bohème (1896), Act I fig 35
Puccini [4']

*Paris, 1830: Rodolfo asks Mimì, a shy neighbour from upstairs, to tell him about herself. Her real name is Lucia, and she embroiders cloth and silk. Her hobby is making silk flowers and she enjoys all the things that poets dream about – the first kiss of spring is hers because her room overlooks the other roofs. Her silk flowers have no scent – what else can she say?*

A very good audition aria, which shows off the middle voice, good legato and a command of Italian, especially in the last sentence. The aria requires a fresh, spontaneous feeling, and the accompaniment should be rich.

### 42. Donde lieta uscì al tuo grido d'amore (Mimì)
La bohème (1896), Act III fig 26
Puccini [2'30"]

*Paris, 1830: Rodolfo, jealous of Mimì's flirting, has walked out on her, so next morning Mimì comes for help from Marcello at an inn on the outskirts of Paris. Rodolfo has, meanwhile, stayed the night there and overhears him telling Marcello of their miserable life. Her cough gives her away and, after Marcello leaves to find out what Musetta is laughing about, she sings this aria to Rodolfo. She asks that some of her possessions*

*be sent to her as she decided to return to her old way of life, making flowers. He may keep the red bonnet, which is under her pillow, as a token of their past love.*

This aria lies quite low except for the end. It needs a lot of spontaneous feeling to make it interesting.

### 43. Měsíčku na nebi hlubokém –
### Song to the moon (Rusalka)
Rusalka (1901), Act I fig 39
Dvořák [4'10"]

*A lakeside glade, legendary: Rusalka, a nymph and daughter of the Spirit of the Lake, sings to the moon of her love for a mortal stranger – a prince who came to bathe at the lake. Rusalka is warned by the Water Spirit of the dangers of becoming mortal (which she desires in order to be close to the prince). Left alone she confesses her love to the moon.*

Two verses which require sweeping lines and a good mixed tone for the lower notes. All the ornaments need weight of sound. A good singing translation is hard to find because ideally the text should keep to the same note-values as the original. The differences between the two verses should be made very clear.

### 44. Oh! mio babbino caro (Lauretta)
Gianni Schicchi (1918), Fig 44
Puccini [2']

*Florence, 1299: Lauretta, daughter of Gianni Schicchi, is in love with Rinuccio, who is related to Buoso Donati who has just died and left most of his money to charity. The money-grabbing relations have been persuaded by Rinuccio to call in Schicchi, in order to help them find a loophole in the will. When he refuses, Lauretta, on one knee, sings how she loves Rinuccio and wishes to marry him; but now she must throw herself into the Arno. Schicchi, of course, now relents.*

A very short aria, which is ideal for demonstrating legato singing.

**45. Signore ascolta!** (Liù)
Turandot (1926), Act I fig 42
Puccini [2'10"]

*Peking, antiquity: Liù tries to persuade Calaf not to challenge Turandot to the riddle contest.*

A short aria with long slow lines and a difficult high B♭ at the end. The portamentos must be well integrated into the legato line and the accompaniment richly sustained.

**46. Tu, che di gel sei cinta** (Liù)
Turandot (1926), Act III sc 1 fig 27
Puccini [2'10"]

*Peking, antiquity: Calaf has won the riddle contest but has challenged Turandot to discover his name before dawn. Liù is arrested but refuses to tell Turandot the secret, singing that she will take it to the grave. Thereupon she grabs a dagger and stabs herself.*

This is a short aria with rich slow lines and a strong ending. It should be approached in much the same way as the preceding aria (No. 45).

**47. Embroidery Aria** (Ellen)
Peter Grimes (1945), Act III sc 1 fig 23
Britten [3'10"]

*Borough, East Coast of England, c.1830: Ellen, a schoolmistress, has been told by Balstrode, a retired skipper, that although Peter's boat is in, there is no sign of him or his apprentice boy whom Peter is suspected of maltreating. On the shore, Ellen has found the boy's jersey with her embroidered anchor on it. She muses on how her embroidery, which once appealed to children's imagination, has become a terrible clue in the search for Peter and the boy.*

This aria demands control of a slow, weaving line, excellent breath control and the ability at times to sing with a detached expression. The pianist should be fully aware of the orchestration in order to avoid the continuous chords becoming repetitive.

**48. Do not utter a word** (Vanessa)
   Vanessa (1958), Act I fig 22 to 27
   Barber [2'50"]

*A northern country, c.1905: Vanessa has waited 20 years for Anatol's return to her secluded country house in the far north. As he walks in, she dares not look at him, in case the sight of him will change her feeling of love and make him leave again. Not until after this aria does she find out that this is Anatol's son with the same name.*

An aria which has sweeping lines and difficult phrasing. An agitated feeling of restrained emotion is necessary. The best place to end is at 'All this I have done for you', which is at the end of a useful fast section.

# Dramatic coloratura soprano

**49. D'Oreste, d'Ajace!** (Electra)
   (Recit: Oh smania! Oh furie!)
   Idomeneo (1781), Act III no 24 or 29
   Mozart [5'10"] 📖 EP1127

*Crete, after the Trojan Wars: Electra, a Greek princess, is jealously in love with the King of Crete's son, Idamante, who loves a Trojan prisoner, Ilia. At the end of the opera, Neptune releases Idomeneo from his vow to sacrifice his son, and everyone rejoices except Electra. She vents her fury on all the gods.*

A high dramatic aria, which is full of anger. It requires much stamina, especially at the top of the voice. Let the accompaniment provide all the fast energy and allow the voice to sweep over the phrases as if Electra is creating an incantation.

**50. Ach ich liebte, war so glücklich** (Konstanze)
   Die Entführung aus dem Serail (1782), Act I no 6
   Mozart [5'] 📖 EP4231A

*Turkey, 16th century: The Pasha tells Konstanze he is still determined to win her love, but she reminds him of her own true love for someone else and how she can only live in dark despair until she regains him.*

A high, cantabile aria requiring stamina in this range; it must sound smooth and enticing. There should be a tempo relation between the Adagio and the Allegro (i.e. quaver equals crotchet), in order that the return of the first set of words is at the same tempo. Of all Konstanze's arias this is probably the most difficult to sing, so be very certain of it technically.

**51. Or sai chi l'onore** (Donna Anna)
(Recit: Allora rinforzo i stridi miei)
Don Giovanni (1787), Act I no 10
Mozart [3'45"] 📖 EP8901

*Seville, 17th century: Donna Anna has just described to Don Ottavio, her betrothed, how she has realized that Don Giovanni was the unknown man who attacked her. She asks Don Ottavio to exact vengeance on the assailant.*

The range of this aria often lies around high G and A, so you must be very secure in this part of your voice. It helps to begin at the end of the accompanied recitative, which will also demonstrate a short passage of dramatic narration. The aria requires good line, letting the orchestra convey the feeling of vengeance. There are essentially three dramatic elements (three musical ideas are similarly juxtaposed) which have to be communicated – Donna Anna's triumph at discovering who killed her father, her appeal for vengeance, and lastly the remembrance of the horrible crime.

**52. Non mi dir, bell'idol mio** (Donna Anna)
(Recit: Crudele!)
Don Giovanni (1787), Act II no 25
Mozart [6'10"] 📖 EP8901, EP4231A, EP734

*Seville, 17th century: Donna Anna is delaying her marriage to Don Ottavio because she feels that public opinion will consider it is too soon*

*after Don Giovanni's outrage against her. She calms Don Ottavio by saying that she is not cruel and needs compassion both from him and from heaven.*

This aria is quite long and, like 'Or sai chi l'onore', lies high, around G and A. The recitative and aria contain extremely long phrases, which require stunning breath control. The second part contains difficult coloratura, which illustrates Donna Anna's appeal to heaven, as if 'on wings'. The ending is big and demands careful management. At the end of the recitative, at the word 'abbastanza', opinion is divided as to whether Mozart intended an A♭ or an A♮ on the descending phrase. Decide which you prefer and make your choice very clear.

**53. Come scoglio** (Fiordiligi)
(Recit: Temerari)
Così fan tutte (1790), Act I no 14
Mozart [5'10"] 📖 EP4231A

*Naples, 18th century: Fiordiligi reacts against the two wooing Albanians (the sisters' lovers in disguise) by delivering a strong lecture about how her constant faithfulness to her love can be compared to a firm rock.*

A good audition aria showing off a wide range with big leaps, though there may not be time for the panel to hear a second aria. A strong recitative is followed by a solid aria, with some coloratura and a final section with difficult runs. The three different tempos should be clearly defined. Make sure that all the phrases begin with a feeling of an upbeat – the Italian text will give you the clue.

**54. O zitt're nicht, mein lieber Sohn!**
(Königen der Nacht)
Die Zauberflöte (1791), Act I no 4
Mozart [4'35"] 📖 EP71

*Egypt, legendary: The Queen of the Night welcomes Tamino and tells him of his task to rescue her daughter, Pamina, from the snares of Sarastro.*

A famous coloratura aria, which is harder than the Queen's second aria, because the only top F arrives unprepared. More time to prepare for the top note can be achieved, if necessary, by omitting the first G and F♯ in the bar before. The aria also needs a rich middle voice and dramatic fire in the story-telling of the abduction. The tempo of the Allegro moderato should be determined by the speed of the coloratura.

**55. Der Hölle Rache** (Königen der Nacht)
Die Zauberflöte (1791), Act II no 14
Mozart [3'10"] 📖 EP4231A, EP2074

*Egypt, legendary: The Queen of the Night visits her daughter in Sarastro's temple and finds that Tamino has joined the initiates. She tells Pamina that the only way to escape is by killing Sarastro with a dagger. She sings of her vengeance.*

A coloratura aria, which is easier to negotiate than the Queen's first aria but does not show off as many colours of the voice; it may therefore be better to choose the first aria for audition purposes. The ending should be sung very dramatically, giving the feeling of an accompanied recitative.

**56. Bel raggio lusinghier** (Semiramide)
Semiramide (1823), Act I no 7
Rossini [6' shortened intro. and playout] 📖 EP2074

*Babylon, antiquity: Semiramide, the Queen of Babylon, awaits her supposed lover, Arsace, a general in her army. As she hears him coming, she sings of her joy and how all her sorrows now fly away.*

This is a coloratura aria, which tends to stay in the same range and has many difficult runs. The second verse of the Allegretto should be ornamented and some of the coda can be cut. (See Ricci, *Book of Cadenzas*.)

**57. Ocean! thou mighty monster** (Reiza)
Oberon (1826), Act II no 13
Weber [8'45"] 📖 EP734

*Rocky seashore, legendary: Reiza, the Caliph of Bagdad's daughter, has escaped through the help of Oberon's magic with her lover, Sir Huon. They are shipwrecked by a storm raised by Puck and his elements. While Sir Huon goes for help, Reiza, on the shore, describes the storm abating, the sun setting and finally a boat approaching, which she imagines has come to rescue them.*

A dramatic recitative, which is very long, and an aria with a difficult ending, including the tricky name of Huon. This opera was originally written in English by J. R. Planché, and helps to solve the difficulty of finding an audition aria in English. The aria demonstrates Weber's style very well, but can also be heard to foreshadow Wagner's music, which could be helpful in an audition. In the fourth bar before the Allegro moderato a high B♭ can be sung instead of the F. The portrayal of the forces of nature and the boat approaching must be well coloured in the contrasting sections.

## 58. **Casta diva** (Norma)
(Cabaletta: Ah! bello a me ritorna)
Norma (1831), Act I no 4
Bellini [5'15" short intro. + 2'30" one verse]  EP734, EP2074, EP4231B

*Gaul, c.50 BC: Norma, the high priestess of the Druids, sings an invocation to the moon. In the cabaletta, she sings of her secret love for a Roman proconsul named Pollione. She appeals to him to return to her and restore the beauty of their first love.*

A famous cavatina, which demonstrates smooth and effortless singing, perfectly executed melismas and control of chromatic runs. The cabaletta contains some very difficult coloratura. Cut from the end of the cavatina straight to the cabaletta, and from here sing the second verse. (See Ricci, *Book of Cadenzas*.)

**59. Ah! non credea mirarti** (Amina)

(Cabaletta: Ah! non giunge)

La sonnambula (1831), Act III no 14

Bellini [3'30" + 1'45" cut]  EP2074

Cavatina:  Cabaletta:

*Switzerland, early-19th century: Amina, due to a misunderstanding caused by her secret sleepwalking, has been rejected by her lover Elvino. Now the villagers have seen her sleepwalking during the day and realize the truth. In the cavatina she sings of how flowers are as transient as her love. When Elvino replaces the ring on Amina's finger, she sings the cabaletta about her joy at their reunion.*

A beautiful, sad cavatina in which Amina's wandering mind needs to be suggested through a smooth, simple line and a silvery tone, similar to the beauty of a Chopin nocturne. In the cabaletta, Amina's recovery must be demonstrated by the virtuosity of the coloratura and the jumps. After the cavatina, begin directly at the cabaletta, singing only one verse. At the Più vivo, cut to the final four complete bars of singing. (See Ricci, *Book of Cadenzas.*)

**60. Regnava nel silenzio** (Lucia)

(Cabaletta: Quando rapito in estasi)

Lucia di Lammermoor (1835), Act I sc 2

Donizetti [3'10" + 4'15" cut interlude] EP2074

Cavatina:  Cabaletta:

*Scotland, 1700: By a fountain, Lucia fearfully reminds her lady-in-waiting, Alisa, of the incident which happened at this spot. One of the Ravenswood family, burning with jealousy, stabbed his loved one here and she fell into the water. Now her ghost has appeared to Lucia, the water seeming to turn to blood. Alisa feels that this ghostly appearance indicates a bad omen for Lucia's love for Edgardo Ravenswood, but Lucia remains fully convinced of her affection.*

The cavatina must have strong elements of a narration of a ghost story. In complete contrast, the cabaletta should be a joyful brilliant aria demonstrating absolute faith in Edgardo's love. The transition, after the cavatina, needs to be shortened to a few bars before 'Egli è luce'. Also, singing both verses of the cabaletta allows you to vary the ornamentation – at the end an optional high D can be inserted. The interlude between the two verses of the cabaletta should be shortened and, at the Poco più, a cut made to the last four complete bars of singing (see Ricci, *Book of Cadenzas*). The coloratura can be sung imaginatively to illustrate the respective words. The pianist should check the accompaniment with the full score as the bass line is sometimes transcribed incorrectly.

**61. Qui la voce sua soave** (Elvira)
(Cabaletta: Vien, diletto)
I puritani (1835), Act II fig 24
Bellini [2'35" + 2'30" one verse, short playout] 📖 EP2074

*Plymouth, The English Civil War: Elvira's intended bridegroom Arturo has escaped with an unknown lady wearing a bridal veil. This shock has driven Elvira mad, and Riccardo and Giorgio are witness to her wanderings. In the cavatina she hears a distant voice calling to her, swearing loyalty, but now he has forsaken her. She pleads for a sign of hope or she must die. In the cabaletta, she sees Arturo in her mind and draws him towards her.*

The cavatina needs a steady, pure tone to suggest Elvira's madness. The cabaletta is full of virtuoso coloratura and brilliance. It is best to begin at 'Qui la voce' without the introductory phrases. Sing only one verse of the cabaletta and end with the last phrase containing a high C. (See Ricci, *Book of Cadenzas*.) The music between the cavatina and cabaletta (i.e. between figures 26 and 36) would obviously be cut.

**62. Il faut partir** (Marie)
La fille du régiment (1840), Act I no 13
Donizetti [2'45" one verse]

*Swiss Tyrol, 1815: Marie, the regiment's adopted daughter, has discovered that the Marquise de Birkenfield, who has demanded a military escort for her travels, is her aunt. She is required to accompany her back to their ancestral home, so she sadly bids farewell to the regiment.*

A beautiful cavatina, which shows off legato singing. It is best to sing only one verse followed by the stretto with the chorus.

**63. Ernani! Ernani, involami** (Elvira)
(Recit: Sorta è la notte)
(Cabaletta: Tutto sprezzo, che d'Ernani)
Ernani (1844), Act I fig 16
Verdi [3'45" + 2' one verse]  EP4246A

*Spain, early-16th century: Elvira, due to be married to Don Ruy Gomez di Silva, a Grandee of Spain, is secretly in love with a bandit chief, Ernani. In her apartment at night, waiting for Silva, she sings in the recitative that she hopes he will not return, for her love for Ernani deepens. In the cavatina, she hopes Ernani will take her away to her dream of love. Before the cabaletta, maidens bring marriage flowers, and Elvira tells how the only things she loves now are those concerned with Ernani.*

This is a very wide-ranging coloratura aria full of dramatic leaps and runs. The first word of the recitative is often misprinted as 'surta'; it should be 'sorta' meaning 'risen'. Only one verse is needed for the cabaletta. The coloratura should be elegantly executed without too much attack or weight.

**64. Verführer!** (Frau Fluth/Mrs Ford)
(Recit: Nun eilt herbei)
Die lustigen Weiber von Windsor (1849),
    Act I sc 2 no 3
Nicolai [5'50" with cut]  EP4231B

*Windsor, c.1400: Falstaff has written to two married ladies, Mrs Page and Mrs Ford, declaring his love for both of them. The two ladies have compared letters and declare revenge. In this scene, after Mrs Ford has told her jealous husband in an anonymous letter about the arranged rendezvous, she is waiting for Falstaff and practising how she will address him, laughing at the tricks that she plays on men.*

Quite a long recitative and aria with virtuoso runs, requiring lots of character and caricature. It is good for auditions as it shows off varying styles – you can add a high C in the run in bar six of the Larghetto. Humour is very apparent, even in the orchestral scale at the end, which reaches top F while the singer sings only up to B♭! The Poco meno mosso should have a Viennese feeling. A cut can be made from the Poco più mosso to the last 25 bars of the music.

**65. Ah, fors'è lui** (Violetta)
(Recit: È strano!)
(Cabaletta: Sempre libera)
La traviata (1853), Act I no 6
Verdi [5'45"]  📖 EP4246B

*Paris, 1850: Violetta, a courtesan, has been left alone by her party guests after feeling unwell. A stranger, Alfredo, stayed behind to comfort her and, after he leaves, she muses on this new, strange feeling she is experiencing – could she be seriously in love? At 'A quell'amor … ' she recalls some of the phrases he sang to her. She brings herself back to the present by saying that it is all folly and delusion: it is better to remain in this life of whirlwind pleasure and sensuality. Even when Alfredo sings outside her window, she forces herself to retain this delusion of joy.*

A long aria, of which only one verse each of the cavatina and cabaletta should be sung. It contains many facets and colours, and demonstrates the voice admirably. All the ornaments should give a feeling of spontaneity and *joie de vivre*. Notice that the last cadenza in the recitative is marked 'Allegro'. The first D♭ of the cavatina should be unexpectedly dissonant. In the cabaletta, the staccatos are an indication of clear text and the repeated A♭ at the end should be re-voiced and not too detached. Do not try the optional top E♭ at the end unless absolutely confident that it will sound easy, for it is not obligatory.

**66. Mercè, dilette amiche** (Elena)
I vespri Siciliani (1855), Act V fig 12
Verdi [2'40" one verse]

*Palermo, 1282: The Duchess of Elena, sister of the Duke of Austria, is due to be married to a young Sicilian called Arrigo. Both of them are involved in a revolution against the French occupation of Sicily. She thanks the chorus for their presentation of flowers, and sings of her future happiness.*

A very hard coloratura aria requiring extreme vitality and a good range. Only the first verse needs to be sung, then cut to figure 17 for the coda. The original language is French, but the aria is now usually sung in Italian.

**67. Ah, je ris de me voir – Air des bijoux** (Marguerite)
(Recit: Ô Dieu)
Faust (1859), Act III no 9
Gounod [4'45"] 📖 EP7552

*Germany, 16th century: Marguerite discovers a casket of jewels, left by Faust with Mephistopheles's help. She puts on the jewels, admiring herself in a mirror. Only at one point in the aria does she feel a suggestion of evil.*

This aria demands sparkle, personality and easy agility. Marguerite's reactions should be naïvely spontaneous. It is best to begin in the recitative. There is a danger that this piece can sound rather laboured because of the frequency of barlines and the quantity of words, so you need to sing with as much fluidity as possible.

**68. L'altra notte in fondo al mare** (Margerita)
Mefistofele (1868), Act III
Boito [3'15"]

*Germany, 16th century: Margerita, lying in prison half-mad, sings of her nightmare in which she drowned her child.*

This aria demands a rich voice throughout its range, the low notes included. It also requires emotional stamina and good coloratura. The impression of madness comes from the changes in style of singing within each verse. See Ricci, *Book of Cadenzas* for a different underlay for the cadenza on 'vola' and for the correct last phrase. Each verse should end with the text 'Ah! di me pietà!'.

**69. Klänge der Heimat – Csárdás** (Rosalinde)
Die Fledermaus (1874), Act II no 10
Johann Strauss [4']  📖 EP9777

*Vienna, late-19th century: Rosalinde has arrived at Prince Orlofsky's party disguised as a Hungarian countess. She first discovers her husband, Eisenstein, who should have been in prison, and secondly her maid, Adele, clothed in one of her mistress's dresses. Adele asks if she is really Hungarian; Rosalinde replies by singing this Csárdás, all about the music of her homeland (this makes her cry), and the glorious countryside. In the Frischka she calls on all patriots to dance away the night while drinking Tokay together.*

A coloratura, virtuoso aria, which demands much extrovert singing. It is best to make a cut in the Frischka from figure 5 to figure 6 (i.e. cut bars 17–32).

**70. No word from Tom – Cavatina** (Anne Truelove)
(Cabaletta: My Father!)
The Rake's Progress (1951), Act I sc 3 fig 179
Stravinsky [3'45" + 4'15"]

*England, 18th century: Tom Rakewell, Anne's love, has gone to London with Nick Shadow and, although Anne has heard nothing, she feels he needs her help. She is about to travel to London late at night without her father's knowledge. She asks the night to find and comfort Tom and hopes the moon will guide her to his cold heart. Her father calls to her, which reminds Anne that he is strong while Tom is weak and needs her. Love will not alter, in spite of what she may find in Tom.*

A long audition aria needing no other aria to go with it, although you can choose to sing either the cavatina or the cabaletta (with its difficult final high C) and its appropriate recitative. It contains a mixture of everything – wide range, legato singing, coloratura, declamatory singing, diction and character. The points at which you breathe must be carefully worked out. At figure 188 in the cavatina Stravinsky gave an alternative word underlay: 'He' on E, 'wat-' on G and F♯, '-ches' on C♯, 'with-' on E and '-out' on D. Make sure the correct stress of the English text is allowed to come through across the beat and, as in Mozart, the singer should sing clearly the phrasing of the vocal line against the 'backing' of the accompaniment. The cabaletta is very hard for the pianist.

# Spinto soprano

**71. Divinités du Styx** (Alceste)
Alceste (1776), Act I sc 7
Gluck [3'50"] 📖 EP734, EP4231A

*Thessaly, antiquity: Admete, King of Thessaly, is near to death, and the oracle has pronounced that his life can only be saved if a friend dies in his place. Without Admete's knowledge, his wife Alceste has offered up her life and now prepares for death. As she defies the Furies of Hell she is filled with strength and courage.*

This is a demanding Baroque aria which has dramatic phrases and a surprisingly wide range. If you keep the feeling of one pulse to a bar it will help to give a forward intention to the phrasing. The original Vienna version of 1767 was in Italian.

**72. Leise, leise** (Agathe)
(Recit: Wie nahte mir der Schlummer)
Der Freischütz (1821), Act II no 8
Weber [8'] 📖 EP4231B

*Bohemia, 17th century: On a starry night, Agathe is waiting in her room for her lover, Max. She goes out on to the balcony to pray that God will guide her in everything. She listens and hears some footsteps, and then imagines that he has won the shooting match and will be wearing a flowery wreath in his hat to denote success. The last section demonstrates her ecstatic anticipation of their meeting.*

A very long aria containing a recitative, cavatina, recitative, Andante, recitative and a Vivace con fuoco. It lies mostly in the middle of the voice except for the last section, which demands great flexibility. You could cut from the end of the first Adagio straight to the Andante.

**73. Dich, teure Halle** (Elizabeth)
Tannhäuser (1845), Act II
Wagner [3'20"] 📖 EP734

*Wartburgner Eisenach, early-13th century: On hearing the news that Tannhäuser has agreed, out of love for Elizabeth, not to go on a pilgrimage to Rome to ask forgiveness for his association with Venus, Elizabeth greets the singer's hall where she first saw him. She sings of how the hall has been joyless while he has been away, but now he is returning, new life will return.*

This aria has declamatory, long phrases which demonstrate the voice well. The phrase 'aus mir entfloh der Frieden' is especially testing.

**74. Einsam in trüben Tagen – Elsa's Dream** (Elsa)
Lohengrin (1850), Act I fig 15
Wagner [5'40"] 📖 EP734

*Brabant (Antwerp), first half of 10th century: Elsa has been accused by Friedrich Telramund, Count of Brabant, of murdering her brother, Godfrey, who was the rightful heir to the dukedom. Before Heinrich, King of Germany, she is asked to defend herself. At first she is silent, but then, as in a dream, tells how after praying fervently she felt her prayers reach up to heaven. She fell into a deep sleep and dreamt she saw a wonderful knight who gave her comfort. He will be her defender against this accusation.*

This aria contains a slow, declamatory voice part over a melodic line in the orchestra. You need good control of the German text at the slow tempo. There is a cut after 'Er soll mein Streiter sein!' to the orchestral tune before the repeat of 'Des Ritters will ich wahren'.

**75. Tacea la notte placida** (Leonora)
(Cabaletta: Di tale amor)
Il trovatore (1853), Act I no 4
Verdi [3'30" + 1'50"]

*Aragon, 15th century: Leonora confides in Inez that she is secretly in love with an unknown knight who left for war. Since then she has heard a lute and a troubadour's song in which he sang her name. She saw him before her window and felt she was in heaven. Before the cabaletta, Inez pleads with her to forget him. Leonora says there is no love like this and, if she cannot live for him, then she must die for him.*

A very difficult aria, which needs changes to the underlay of the text in order to make it easier. Cut straight from the cavatina to the cabaletta, and then sing only one verse. (See Ricci, *Book of Cadenzas*.)

**76. Ten lásky sen, jak krásný byl!** (Mařenka)
(Recit: Och! jaký žal!)
Prodaná Nevěsta (The Bartered Bride)
    (1866), Act III sc 6
Smetana [4'50"]

*Bohemia, 19th century: Kecal, a marriage-broker, has arranged for Mařenka to marry Vašek, a stammering, simple lad. Mařenka loves Jeník, but he has signed a document for Kecal in return for payment, which ensures that Mařenka will marry Vašek. When faced with this document, Mařenka asks to be left alone to think. She wonders how Jeník could mock her by signing the document: if only she could find out the whole truth. In the aria, she muses on how their love could have been, and cannot believe he could leave her alone like this.*

A short recitative followed by a rich aria with long lines. The voice must sound young and yet full-bodied. The singer should be always aware of the underlying continuous melody in the orchestra.

**77. Suicidio!** (La Gioconda)
La Gioconda (1876), Act IV
Ponchielli [3'20"]

*Venice, 17th century: Enzo, whom La Gioconda loves, has fallen in love with Laura, wife of Alvise, head of the Inquisition in Venice. Laura saved Gioconda's blind mother, Cieca, from imprisonment and, because of her suspected adultery, Laura was forced to take poison. Gioconda saved her life by switching the poison for a narcotic, which causes a death-like state, and bringing her body to her deserted house. Meanwhile, Enzo has been imprisoned for threatening the life of Alvise, and Cieca is nowhere to be found. In this aria, Gioconda expresses the horror of it all and considers suicide.*

A heavy, dramatic aria full of contrasts, requiring good lower notes. The phrases in the final section 'domando al ciel' must be carefully shaped so that they do not drag.

**78. Pleurez! Pleurez, mes yeux!** (Chimène)
(Recit: De cet affreux combat)
Le Cid (1885), Act III fig 228
Massenet [4'45"]  EP7552

*Spain, 12th century: Chimène's father Don Gormas has been slain in a duel by Rodrigo (Le Cid – the conqueror), because Rodrigo felt duty-bound to avenge the honour of his father, Don Diego. Don Diego had come off badly some time ago in a quarrel with Don Gormas over a matter of a bestowed position given to Don Diego. Chimène, now that she is alone after this terrible fight, feels she can suffer and cry. She asks the dead if they really need all this relentless suffering.*

A dramatic, rich aria full of sweeping phrases. The French text needs to be sung with full vowels to achieve the intensity of emotion displayed within this piece.

**79. Piangea cantando – Willow Song** (Desdemona)
Otello (1887), Act IV letter E to Q
Verdi [6']

*Cyprus, end of 15th century: Desdemona prepares for bed with the help of her maid, Emilia. She tells of her uneasy premonitions about Othello's arrival, and she is reminded of her mother's maid, Barbara, who sang a song about a girl weeping like a willow tree because a man had deserted her.*

An aria of lamentation and yet with a background of agitation. The lower part of the voice must be very secure to cope with the low notes. There should be much contrast between the longing phrases of the song and the nervous agitation of the recitative-like passages. The pianist should end eight bars before letter Q.

**80. Voi lo sapete, o mamma** (Santuzza)
Cavalleria rusticana (1890), No. 5 (Romanza)
Mascagni [3'40"] 📖 EP4231B

*Sicily, 1890: Santuzza tells Turiddu's mother why she told her to be silent when Alfio spoke of Turiddu. Lola had been in love with Turiddu, but while he was away at war, she married Alfio. Since then, Santuzza has fallen in love with Turiddu, but Lola's old passion has been rekindled and Santuzza has lost Turiddu to Lola.*

This is a demanding, heavy aria, full of emotional weight. It is best to end at 'io son dannata'. In the last phrase of 'io piango' the voice moves up to A on the pause with the oboe.

**81. Uzh polnoch blizitsya** (Lisa)
Queen of Spades (1890), Act III sc 2 no 20
Tchaikovsky [4']

*St Petersburg, end of 18th century: Lisa has forgiven her lover, Hermann, for causing her grandmother's death, and has arranged a meeting by the canal. As midnight approaches, she wonders if he will come. She is tired out from all her anxiety; before, her life brought her happiness – now all her hopes are destroyed.*

An aria with a dramatic opening followed by an Andante with broad phrases. It demonstrates a rich, middle voice. It should be performed with concentrated, intense emotion, but without allowing the voice to become too heavy.

## 82. In quelle trine morbide (Manon Lescaut)
Manon Lescaut (1893), Act II fig 6
Puccini [2']

*Paris, second half of 18th century: Manon has left Des Grieux and is living with a rich man, Geronte. When Lescaut, her cousin, comes to visit her, she tells how all these rich furnishings leave her cold. She still remembers her original, humble dwelling and her lover's ardent caresses.*

This short, slow aria demonstrates a wide range and wonderful line. The voice must guide the tempo at the beginning against the offbeat chords of the woodwind. It is important to try and achieve the *senza rallentando* at the end.

## 83. Sola ... perduta ... abbandonata ...
   (Manon Lescaut)
Manon Lescaut (1893), Act IV fig 10
Puccini [4'15"]

*Louisiana, second half of 18th century: Manon and Des Grieux are in the American desert near the border of New Orleans. Manon had been exiled from France after Geronte had accused her of being a prostitute. Lescaut, her cousin, and Des Grieux attempted to free her before she boarded the prison ship but, after their failure, Des Grieux joined her in her exile. As he goes to look for help, she sings this aria asking that she should die.*

This is a useful aria for showing off a big voice. It requires a good lower voice and a dramatic top. You must communicate that Manon is very close to losing her senses, and this is demonstrated by the sudden changes of mood.

## 84. La mamma morta (Maddalena)
Andrea Chénier (1896), Act III fig 23
Giordano [4']

*Paris, French Revolution: Maddalena's love, Chénier, has been arrested for being a traitor and for wounding Gérard during a duel. Maddalena is brought in to see Gérard and pleads for Chénier's life, which depends on*

*Gérard's evidence. She offers her love in exchange and then, in this aria, describes how her mother was killed and her house burnt. Her maid had become a prostitute to keep them solvent. Only the voice of a god kept her going: its name was Love.*

The recitative lies quite low but the aria slowly climbs in long phrases. It is best to end at the word 'l'amor'. In the Andantino, let the phrase sweep through the barlines following the pulse of the text. Ensure that the final high B is secure after its difficult approach.

**85. Io son l'umile ancella** (Adriana Lecouvreur)
Adriana Lecouvreur (1902), Act I fig 13
Cilea [2'30"]

*Paris, 1730: Adriana, a famous actress at the Comédie Française, is preparing to go on stage. She is overheard rehearsing her lines by the Prince of Bouillon and the Abbot of Chazeuil. To their words of praise she humbly replies that she is merely the servant of the creative genius which flows through her.*

This is a short aria with a wonderful, melodic line. It needs good use of portamentos and rich tone for the lower notes. It is best to begin at the phrase 'Ecco: respiro appena'.

**86. Un bel dì, vedremo** (Madama Butterfly)
Madama Butterfly (1904), Act II fig 12
Puccini [4']

*Nagasaki, 1900: Pinkerton, Butterfly's American husband, promised to return when the robins nest, but it has been three years now. Suzuki, her servant, is losing faith, but Butterfly is steadfast and insists that Suzuki repeats that he will return. Suzuki breaks down. In this aria, Butterfly describes the day when she will see a wisp of smoke on the horizon and a ship will appear. She won't go and meet it, but will wait and see the little figure appear from the town and start climbing the hill. He will call her name but she will hide, partly to tease him but also not to faint with joy. Suzuki must not fear, but must await him with steadfast courage.*

An imaginative aria, with long phrases, requiring good control at the lowest part of the voice's range. It is possible to begin at the phrase 'Piangi? Perchè?' which makes it easier to prepare the *pianissimo* start of the aria. Butterfly's vision of her meeting with Pinkerton needs to be imaginatively and magically communicated, especially the feeling of distance and his gradual approach.

**87. Senza mamma, o bimbo** (Suor Angelica)
Suor Angelica (1918), Fig 60
Puccini [4']

*Cloisters of a nunnery, 17th century: Angelica's aunt, La Principessa, has just visited her in the convent and has told her that she must remain in holy orders to atone for her sin of being an unmarried mother. Angelica asks after her child, only to be told that he died two years ago. After her aunt has left, Angelica sings this lament for her child, who died without knowing a mother's love. Now the boy is in heaven, Angelica longs to be with him and asks when it may be.*

A slow, intense aria which generally lies in the middle range but has a difficult, floating A at the end. It is hard to let the phrases flow and not make them sound laboured – the vision of the boy in heaven must always be kept in mind.

# Dramatic soprano

**88. Abscheulicher! wo eilst du hin?** (Fidelio)
Fidelio (1805), Act I no 9
Beethoven [6'30"] 📖 EP4231A

*Seville, 18th century: Leonore, disguised as a young man called Fidelio, is trying to discover if her husband, Florestan, is being held in prison by his political enemy, Pizarro. She overhears Pizarro ordering the jailer Rocco to prepare a grave for a prisoner held in solitary confinement, who she suspects is her husband. Her monologue shows all her troubled reactions, but she finds consolation and hope in her constant love for Florestan. In the cabaletta she is determined not to flinch from her destined task.*

A heavy, demanding aria consisting of a dramatic recitative, a sustained, long cavatina, then a virtuoso cabaletta with difficult, climbing phrases up to high B. The German text needs well-sung vowels and good line. Even when the phrases descend there must be no loss of ecstatic fervour. Feel the final section in one in a bar and leave the orchestra to provide the throbbing heartbeat.

**89. Ecco l'orrido campo** (Amelia)
Un ballo in maschera (1859), Act II fig 6
Verdi [6'10" short intro.]

*Sweden, 1792: Amelia is married to Gustavo's (Riccardo's) secretary, Count Anckarstroem (Renato), but has fallen in love with the king. She has gone to Mme Arvidson (Ulrica) to find a cure for this love, and she is sent to a terrible place where criminals are hanged, to pick a magic herb at the hour of midnight. There she describes the horrors of her surroundings, and tries to face up to them and also to death. She hopes the herb will annihilate her secret love but still finds herself fighting her fear. Hearing the midnight bell, she sees a staring head come out of the ground. She calls on God to protect her.*

A very dramatic aria containing recitative, cavatina with cor anglais solo, declamatory Allegro and a short recapitulation of the cavatina. It requires a big and wide-ranging voice and has a difficult high C near the end. See Ricci, *Book of Cadenzas* for an alternative final cadenza.

**90. Madre, pietosa vergine** (Leonora)
(Recit: Son giunta! …)
La forza del destino (1862), Act II sc 2 no 12
Verdi [6'20"]

*Spain, 18th century: Leonora was escaping from her home with her lover when her father was accidentally killed by her lover's pistol. She arrives at a monastery seeking sanctuary, and she prays for forgiveness of her sins and finds courage in the sound of the monks singing the Venite.*

The highly dramatic recitative can make this aria too long. The aria is very rich and demanding and, like the recitative, requires a good lower range and a stunning high B in the recitative. The text is set quite slowly so it needs good, long vowels.

**91. Pace, mio Dio** (Leonora)
La forza del destino (1862), Act IV sc 2 no 33
Verdi [5'20"]

*Spain, 18th century: Leonora has been lodged in a secluded grotto within a monastery grounds to secrete her from her avenging brother. She prays for peace, which she feels will be a vain hope, and despairs of ever meeting her lover again. The bread left for her will prolong these terrible days. She is suddenly interrupted by the sound of someone approaching and she curses this profanation of a sacred place.*

An aria with long, sustained lines, demanding a rich voice, and a good high B♭. The pianist should keep the triplet quavers in the accompaniment light to sound like the harp. The rhythm of the second and third 'fatalità', like Beethoven's Fifth Symphony, should be clearly enunciated as with the orchestral introduction – it returns in the 'maledizione' at the end; you can finish with an extra 'maledizion' up to the final B♭, on three crotchets.

**92. Vieni! t'affretta** (Lady Macbeth)
(Recit: Ambizioso spirto)
(Cabaletta: Or tutti sorgete)
Macbeth (1847/1865), Act I sc 2 no 4
Verdi [4'10" + 2'40" one verse]

*Scotland, 1040: Lady Macbeth has just read a letter from her husband telling of his meeting with the witches, and that their prophecy of his gaining the title of Cawdor has come true. In the cavatina, she soliloquizes about her ambition that Macbeth should go further and gain the crown. A messenger announces that the king will stay the night in their castle. In the cabaletta she foresees the fateful advantages of the king's visit for the realization of her ambition.*

A big, dramatic aria containing a recitative, cavatina and cabaletta which requires coloratura and a weighty line. Begin after the letter reading at 'Ambizioso spirto' with the pianist playing a two-bar introduction on the E major chord. After the cavatina, cut to four bars before 'Duncano sarà qui?' and sing only the second verse of the cabaletta.

**93. Ritorna vincitor!** (Aida)
Aida (1871), Act I
Verdi [5'45"]

*Memphis, Reign of the Pharaohs: Aida has just heard with joy that her lover, Radames, has been chosen to lead the Egyptian army against the Ethiopians. But then she recalls that she is a slave, and that her father, the king and leader of the Ethiopian army, is fighting to release her from bondage. She foresees with horror the result of Radames's victory but remembers her love for him: her heart is torn apart. She calls to her gods to have pity on her suffering.*

A big, dramatic aria full of contrasts: recitative, cantabile declamation, and a prayer with a wonderful line. The pianist should play the preceding march as an introduction. The middle section 'I sacri nomi' should show the singer's command of all the different Verdi notations – smorzatura accents, *messa di voce* accents, dots indicating clear text ('nè profferir' should have smorzatura accents) – within a short space of time. In the last six bars of the vocal part the word underlay is usually changed – on the turn on the low D♭ is sung the syllable 'del', 'mio' on the C, 'sof-' on the B♭ and '-frir' on the A♭. The final words become 'Numi, pietà del mio soffrir!'.

**94. Vissi d'arte** (Tosca)
Tosca (1900), Act II fig 51
Puccini [2'50"]

*Rome, 1800: As Cavaradossi is tortured to find out where an escaped prisoner is hiding, Tosca, in desperation, tells Scarpia, the police chief, where he is. She pleads for Cavaradossi's life and Scarpia uses it as a pawn for her love. He tries to take her, but the execution drum halts him and he uses it to describe the process of an execution. In the aria, Tosca meditates on her devotion to art and love, and how she secretly helped the poor. She asks God why she is not rewarded for these acts.*

An aria with long cantabile phrases requiring good breath control. Notice, with two exceptions, that all the phrases are marked by Puccini with legato phrase-marks, which means they must not be declaimed.

**95. Es gibt ein Reich** (Ariadne)
Ariadne auf Naxos (1912), fig 60
Richard Strauss [5'15"]

*Island of Naxos, antiquity: Ariadne has been left on Naxos and imagines that this is the land of death. She awaits the Herald of Death, a god of purity compared to the corruption on earth. She will put on festive garments and wait in her cave; but her soul will follow her god and her freedom will be restored. She prays that the burden of life will be lifted.*

This is a big aria with a wide range, requiring vocal stamina, especially for the ending. The last phrase is very hard to sing in tune. Notice that the text falls within a pulse of one in a bar.

# Heavy dramatic soprano

**96. In questa reggia** (Turandot)
Turandot (1926), Act II sc 2 fig 43 to 49
Puccini [6']

*Far East, antiquity: The Princess explains the reason for her hatred of men. Thousands of years before, Princess Lo-u-ling, defeated in battle, was captured and tortured by a stranger – so Turandot has sworn revenge.*

An aria with a strong, solid line demanding a big voice. Every note needs to be fully sung, including the demisemiquavers.

# Mezzo-soprano arias

## Lyric mezzo

**97. Non so più cosa son, cosa faccio** (Cherubino)
(Recit: Leggila alla padrona)
Le nozze di Figaro (1786), Act I no 6
Mozart [2'40"] 📖 EP734, EP4231A

*Seville, 18th century: Cherubino has passionately snatched from Susanna a ribbon from the Countess's night-cap. He offers his own newly composed song (see No. 98) in fair exchange and tells her to sing it to every lady in the place. They all make him tremble with delight: the feeling of love has engulfed him totally.*

This useful aria, which lies around high F, requires a fluid sense of line and a passionate, inspired text delivery, in which the double consonants such as in 'donna' must be beautifully placed and the penultimate 'con me' exquisitely delayed. Be careful that the text is never bumpy or sounds syllabic. It is better to sing the end of the recitative in order to prepare for the beginning of the aria. The Adagio at the end is like an interruption of the preceding passionate flow, as if Cherubino has suddenly become confused.

**98. Voi, che sapete che cosa è amor** (Cherubino)
Le nozze di Figaro (1786), Act II no 11
Mozart [2'30"] 📖 EP4231A, EP734

*Seville 18th century: This is Cherubino's newly composed song that he offered to Susanna in Act I, and is now teasingly asked to sing by Susanna and the Countess. It is about the effect love has on him and the reaction it produces. At the words 'sospiro e gemo' it seems as if Cherubino breaks away from the composed song and then returns, embarrassed, to the original.*

An aria full of varied colours and seductive feeling within the music. The range lies around high F. The melody is very simple and folk-like, giving the impression that Cherubino is using a well-known tune, and the melodic ornaments need to be well sung and projected. As with the other Cherubino aria (No. 97), make sure that the text is smooth and fluid.

**99. Smanie implacabili** (Dorabella)
(Recit: Ah scostati!)
Così fan tutte (1790), Act I no 11
Mozart [3'15"] 📖 EP4232, EP4231A

*Naples, 18th century: In front of her audience, consisting of her sister, Fiordiligi and Despina the maid, Dorabella demonstrates an over-dramatic reaction to the departure of her lover, Ferrando. He and Guglielmo, Fiordiligi's lover, have suddenly been sent off to war. In 'Gluckian' fashion she appeals to the Furies to torture her until she dies.*

An exciting, dramatic aria, requiring a full emotional range of colours. The aria should be like a dialogue between Dorabella and the Furies, who are illustrated by the orchestra.

**100. È amore un ladroncello** (Dorabella)

Così fan tutte (1790), Act II no 28

Mozart [3'] 📖 EP734

*Naples, 18th century: Dorabella humorously encourages her sister, Fiordiligi, to give in to Cupid's designs as she herself intends to do.*

A Despina-like aria with a 6/8 dance feeling. It requires flexibility and good top of the voice. On the repetition of 'che l'anima in catena' the seventh quaver should be a C♯.

**101. Parto, parto, ma tu ben mio** (Sesto)

La clemenza di Tito (1791), Act I no 9

Mozart [6'40"] 📖 EP4232

*Rome, AD 79–81: Vitellia is secretly in love with the Roman Emperor, Titus, and is determined at any cost to stop him from marrying anyone else. She knows Sesto, a Roman patrician, is in love with her, and she persuades him to take part in a plot against the life of Titus. In this aria, Sesto says he will leave and do what she desires, thinking only of his love for her.*

An aria difficult to control, requiring legato singing as good as the clarinet obbligato (originally a corno di basetto which could play a bottom B♭), and much authority. The three sections are each slightly faster and the last section has difficult triplet runs, which need to be well shaped and avoid sounding like a machine gun being fired! In the Allegro section, it would be better to sing 'A questo sguardo solo da me si penserà' rather than 'di quello sguardo solo io me ricorderò'.

**102. Deh per questo istante solo** (Sesto)

La clemenza di Tito (1791), Act II no 19

Mozart [6'30"] 📖 EP4232

*Rome, AD 79–81: Sesto is faced by proof of his involvement in the conspiracy against the Roman Emperor's life. He makes a final speech to Titus, his best friend, recalling their love, and tells how he is only concerned with Titus's contempt for him when he dies. If Titus knew how much he suffered he would be less severe.*

This aria has a small range, which is not too difficult to sing. It is hard, however, to make it sound interesting. In each of the three sections the agitation that Sesto feels in facing death must be progressively increased.

**103. Cruda sorte!** (Isabella)
L'italiana in Algeri (1813), Act I no 4
Rossini [4']

*Algiers, 18th century: Isabella has been shipwrecked on a beach in Algiers where, by chance and unknown to her, her lover is a slave of the Bey. She sings of her cruel fate and asks for help from God. She faces Mustafa's slaves with courage, knowing she has the confidence of a woman's technique in dealing with men.*

This coloratura aria has a slow recitative and a fast section, which lies quite low. It demands much character and control of difficult runs. There should be a feeling of intense danger all around Isabella – thus the aria should not come across as too relaxed.

**104. Una voce poco fa** (Rosina)
Il barbiere di Siviglia (1816), Act I no 5
Rossini [5'30"]    EP794, EP4231B, EP2074, EP734

*Seville, 17th century: Like Gilda, Rosina has just discovered her lover's name and sings that she knows 'Lindoro' will be hers and that she will fool her guardian, Dr Bartolo. In the second part, she describes herself – how she can be sweet and loving and yet change into a viper, playing all the tricks to get her way.*

A good coloratura aria, with many opportunities for 'feline' colours and changes of mood, which demonstrate Rosina's whims. There is endless scope for ornamentation, which should be chosen to suit the meaning of the text and your own interpretation. Allow the coloratura to create the effect of bringing out the text, without adding any accents on the words. A soprano can choose to sing this aria in F major using suitable cadenzas. (See Ricci, *Book of Cadenzas.*)

**105. Nacqui all'affanno e al pianto** (Cenerentola)
(Cabaletta: Non più mesta accanto al fuoco)
La Cenerentola (1817), Act II Rondo finale fig 40
Rossini [6'20"]   📖 EP4232

*Legendary: Cinderella, in a speech before everyone, tells of how her sad fate
has been transformed into a joyful one. She asks her family to dry their
tears (of disappointment) and partake of her happiness in finding her
prince.*

A very florid aria with a big range, needing much personality and verve,
especially with the high coloratura towards the end. The text underlay
in the runs can be adapted to suit your technique. Make a cut of 20
bars in the chorus transition to four bars before the cabaletta, and the
pianist should shorten the playout. (See Ricci, *Book of Cadenzas*.)

**106. Einst träumte meiner sel'gen Base** (Ännchen)
Der Freischütz (1821), Act III no 13
Weber [5'40"]   📖 EP734, EP4231B

*Bohemia, 17th century: On the day of Agathe's wedding, when she will be
betrothed to whoever wins the shooting contest, Agathe has had a bad
dream which bodes ill for her lover, Max. Ännchen, her cousin, attempts to
cheer her up and recounts a story in which things were misinterpreted. A
cousin dreamt that a monster came into her room, but it was only the
watchdog. Agathe is still not convinced, so Ännchen continues saying that
no bride should be unhappy on her wedding day. Tears should be left to the
nuns in the convent.*

Ännchen is a difficult role to cast, as it needs a less noble quality than
Agathe and yet lies in the same range. It can be sung by a lyric coloratura soprano as well as by a lyric mezzo. This is a mock-dramatic
character aria with a 6/8 dance full of runs; these should not go too
fast, partly because of the viola obbligato in the orchestra.

**107. Nobles Seigneurs, salut!** (Urbain)
Les Huguenots (1836), Act I no 5B
Meyerbeer [3'10"]

*Touraine, 1572: Urbain, a page of Queen Marguerite de Valois, arrives at the mansion of the Count de Nevers to ask Raoul de Nangis to attend an unknown lady. He sings of how lucky this man will be to stand before the lady. In actual fact, the queen is making an assignation to persuade Raoul, a Huguenot, to marry Valentine, daughter of a Catholic leader.*

This is a coloratura aria with a 9/8 cantabile aria and showy cadenzas. Most of the phrases begin like an upbeat into a second bar, thus allowing them to flow.

**108. Faites-lui mes aveux** (Siebel)
Faust (1859), Act III no 7
Gounod [3'10"] 📖 EP7553

*Germany, 16th century: Siebel, a youth in love with Marguerite, picks some flowers in her garden for a bouquet. But, as Mephistopheles predicted, they wither. Siebel dips his fingers into a holy font and then gathers more flowers, which this time do not fade.*

This verse, recitative and verse require not only good diction but also fluid phrasing and an easy top to the voice. Lots of colour and quick reactions should be utilized in the recitative.

**109. Connais-tu le pays** (Mignon)
Mignon (1866), Act I no 4
Thomas [4'50"] 📖 EP7553

*Germany, late-18th century: Wilhelm, a young travelling student, asks Mignon, a girl kidnapped at birth and living with the gypsies, some searching questions about the land of which she dreams. She sings the great Goethe poem 'Kennst du das Land', which describes a paradise where she would wish to live, a house on a lake pictured in wonderful detail.*

Two similar verses demanding perfect line and smoothness. The semiquaver, which often occurs within the phrases, should be well resonated and never skipped over. If you find this aria too long, sing only one verse.

**110. Ich lade gern mit Gäste ein** (Orlofsky)
Die Fledermaus (1874), Act II no 7
Johann Strauss [2'45"]  📖 EP9777

*Vienna, late-19th century: Prince Orlofsky, an eccentric rich Russian, tells his guests at his party that, even though he suffers from boredom, he will allow no guest of his to become bored. No one should refuse to drink with him all night or he will throw a bottle at him. 'Chacun à son goût.'*

A two-verse character aria demanding knowledge of style and a good rich lower voice. The top A♭'s should not be clipped.

**111. Ya nye spasobna k'grusti tomnoi** (Olga)
Eugene Onegin (1879), Act I no 3
Tchaikovsky [3'35"]  📖 EP7581

*Russia, late-18th century: Olga tries to persuade her sister, Tatyana, to stop dreaming and to live like Olga, who always enjoys life and is happy.*

An aria full of *joie de vivre* and the sense of teasing an older sister, in the same way as happens between Dorabella and Fiordiligi. It lies quite low and therefore must not sound too heavy, while the pianist must ensure that the difficult accompanying figures are lightly played. Begin at 'Akh, Tanya, Tanya'.

**112. La Maya y el Ruiseñor** (Rosario)
Goyescas (1916), Third tableau
Granados [4'50"]

*Spain, c.1800: Rosario, a highborn lady, waits for her lover, Fernando, in her garden. She sings of the song of the nightingale and how it speaks of love.*

A beautiful, languid aria with wonderful sweeping phrases. It is best to end with the final 'Oh ruiseñor!'.

**113. Must the winter come so soon?** (Erika)
Vanessa (1958), Act I fig 15 to 17
Barber [2'15"]

*A northern country, c.1905: Erika, the 20-year-old niece of Vanessa, who lives in a secluded country house in the far north, sadly asks why the winter always comes so soon.*

A short, tranquil aria requiring good use of text and steady, resonant vowels to help sustain the line.

# Dramatic mezzo

**114. Che farò senza Euridice** (Orfeo)
(Recit: Cara sposa)
Orfeo ed Euridice (1762), Act III no 43
Gluck [4'30"] 📖 EP735

*On the way back from Hades, legendary: This is the lament of Orfeo after he turns to look at his wife, Euridice, who then dies in his arms. He realizes he has caused her death and now asks if there is any point in living. Twice the lament is interrupted, when Orfeo calls out Euridice's name to bring her back, but he calls out in vain.*

An aria with three refrains, the last one extended, interspersed with emotional outbursts. It demands emotional stamina and breadth of tone. Orfeo was originally written for a castrato when performed in Vienna in 1762, but rewritten for a tenor voice (as the aria in F major – 'J'ai perdu mon Euridice') for Paris in 1774, and this version has an extended ending. Although the marking of the underlay of the text sometimes makes the melody seem as if it is phrased in groups of two quavers, the quavers should be grouped together in a single 'bow' to achieve the same phrasing as the melodic line in the orchestra. The pianist is responsible for the strong 'heartbeat' pulse, which continues throughout.

### 115. In sì barbara sciagura (Arsace)

(Si: Vendicato)
Semiramide (1823), Act II no 13
Rossini [3'15" + 3'30"]

*Babylon, antiquity: Arsace, a general in the army of Queen Semiramide of Babylon, has returned home to discover that Semiramide wishes to marry him. Her original consort, Ninus, died in strange circumstances. Oroe, the high priest, has informed Arsace that he is really the son of Ninus and that Semiramide is his mother, and proves it with a written document, showing that Semiramide, with her paramour, Assur, poisoned Ninus. Arsace sings of his hope for consolation and then the chorus exhorts him to take vengeance, to which he agrees. It is right to kill Assur but is it right to kill his own mother? But he realizes that only after vengeance can there be peace.*

This is a low coloratura aria with very difficult runs, in which the fitting in of the syllables must not disturb the line. After the cavatina, make a cut to 'Si, si, Vendetta', the pianist playing the first two bars of the Allegro. At the Allegro vivace, cut to the second verse, preceded by a short six-bar introduction. The coloratura should illustrate the text, and when the runs are sung against the rhythmical accompaniment in the second half, allow them to be well shaped, leaving the orchestra to provide the rhythmic accents.

### 116. O mio Fernando (Leonora)

(Recit: Fia dunque vero!)
La favorita (La favorite) (1840), Act III fig 15
Donizetti [5'50" one verse] 📖 EP7553

*Spain, c.1340: The King of Castile, Alfonso XI, has just permitted his mistress Leonora to marry her real lover, Fernando, who has led the king's army to triumph. In this soliloquy, she gets over the shock of this unexpected news, but then realizes that she cannot stay because of her past relationship with the King. She must let Fernando know all the facts and suffer the consequences for it. In the cabaletta, she says that her suffering will be written in heaven. She is cursed and imagines herself as an unhappy bride, rejected by heaven, wearing a black veil.*

An aria, which is not too high, comprising a dramatic recitative, a cavatina with a seamless line, and a rousing cabaletta, of which only the first verse and coda need be sung. It was originally composed in French. As mentioned earlier, in the comments on background preparation for an audition, it is important to understand the mark > which Donizetti uses with such frequency throughout this aria. It should not be sung like a *sforzando*, which would tire the voice, but sung long with a certain weight of tone. These marks also give a guide to the tessitura of the phrases. (See Ricci, *Book of Cadenzas*.)

**117. Il m'en souvient** (Béatrice)
Béatrice et Bénédict (1862), Act II no 10
Berlioz [4'10" with cut]

*Messina in Sicily, medieval: Béatrice has discovered that Bénédict loves her. She remembers that the day he left with his army she had a strange feeling about him. Now she realizes that she loves him, that she is no longer herself, and that she must say farewell to her frivolous gaiety. She has fallen a victim to love.*

In this virtuoso, showy aria an Andante containing slow lines is followed by an excited, fast aria with high phrases and fast runs. It is best to start at the reprise of the Andante leading into the Allegro agitato 'Je l'aime donc'.

**118. Ah! Je vais mourir** (Didon)
Les troyens (1863), Act V sc 2 no 47
Berlioz [5'35"]  📖 EP7553

*Carthage, after the Trojan Wars: After learning that Aeneas, her lover, has left the country, Dido, the Queen of Carthage, asks to be left alone. She decides to prove her love by dying and letting Aeneas see the funeral flames from his boat. She bids a sad farewell to her country.*

A strong, emotional recitative, followed by a sustained slow aria with long phrases. It requires very disciplined singing. The many E♭'s must sound comfortable, especially the last one.

**119. O don fatale** (Eboli)
Don Carlo (Don Carlos) (1867),
    Act IV sc 1 (5-act version)
Verdi [5'] 📖 EP7553

*Spain, mid-16th century: Princess Eboli, lady-in-waiting to Elisabetta, the wife of King Philip II of Spain, is in love with Don Carlo. In the preceding scene, Eboli jealously hinted that the king should look inside Elisabetta's jewel casket where there is a picture of her lover, also Don Carlo. In this scene the king, in a frightful moment, has denounced Elisabetta before Eboli. This aria is about Eboli's horror at what she has achieved. She blames it on her beauty and curses it. As she bursts into tears, she realizes that a convent is the only place left for her, but remembers that Don Carlo is in prison and is to die tomorrow. Maybe one more day will be enough to save him.*

This is a very high aria, a real tour de force, which demonstrates declamatory power, seamless line and dramatic feeling. The opening section should have the sense of a strong, declamatory recitative. In the aria-like section 'O mia regina' the dynamics can be taken as indications of dramatic contrasts in colour. The original language is French.

**120. So ist es denn aus** (Fricka)
Die Walküre (1870), Act II sc 1 fig 9A
Wagner [3'30"] 📖 EP3404

*Valhalla, legendary: Fricka, Wotan's wife and protector of the marriage vow, angrily denounces Wotan for encouraging the incestuous love between Siegmund and Sieglinde, brother and sister. Wotan devoted his time to the Walküre and now he spends all his time with the race of the Wälsung.*

A declamatory, dramatic aria demanding lots of power and stamina. The outburst of anger must never become a shout but should always be communicated through voice and phrasing. It is best if the pianist begins two bars before the 'Sehr lebhaft'.

### 121. L'amour est un oiseau rebelle
(Habañera) (Carmen)
Carmen (1875), Act I no 5
Bizet [2'50"] 📖 EP7553

*Seville, 1820: The men outside the cigarette factory wait for the girls – especially Carmen – to come out for their morning break. When Carmen arrives, the men ask her for her love, and she replies that love is like a rebellious bird, as free as the wind: but if Carmen decides to love, watch out!*

In this aria it is advisable to cut from the end of the first verse to the four bars of orchestra before the second verse and then cut to the final two bars in order to end the second verse. The aria requires a snake-like line, atmospheric diction and lots of sexual heat.

### 122. Près des remparts de Séville
(Seguidilla) (Carmen)
Carmen (1875), Act I no 10 (or no 9)
Bizet [2'10"] 📖 EP7553

*Seville, 1820: After breaking up a fight among the cigarette girls, Zuniga orders Don José to tie Carmen's hands and take her prisoner to punish her for her insolence. Zuniga then leaves Don José to guard her, but Carmen begins to use all her feminine guile to get herself released. She tells him of a tavern where she will meet her lover ... Don José succumbs to her charms and releases the rope.*

This aria needs a big range and many changes of colour to show all sides of Carmen's character. She must always be a mistress of the subtle suggestion. It is best to cut after the second repetition of 'Près des remparts' to the last time, when its dynamic is 'forte'.

### 123. Amour! Viens aider ma faiblesse! (Dalila)
(Récit: Samson, recherchant ma présence)
Samson et Dalila (1877), Act II sc 1
Saint-Saëns [4'40"] 📖 EP7553

*Gaza, BC: Samson is leading a revolt of the Israelites against their masters, the Philistines. Dalila is sent by the Philistines to seduce him and to find out the secret of his power. Here she awaits him in her house in the valley of Sorek. She asks the God of Love to aid her to entrap Samson.*

A marvellous audition aria, which shows off the entire range, especially in a brilliant, downward scale. It contains recitative, lyrical melody and dramatic declamation. Dalila's faith in her own sexual power must be strongly communicated.

**124. Da, chas nastal!** (Joanna)
The Maid of Orleans (1881), Act I no 7
Tchaikovsky [7'] 📖 EP7581

*France, 1430–31: Joan of Arc has correctly prophesied that the French would defeat the English and that the English leader, Salisbury, would die. After the rejoicing at the news has died down Joan is left alone. She makes the decision to leave home to join the troops, and says farewell to the homeland around her.*

A big, rich aria known by the French title of 'Adieu forêts', it requires strong declamation, solid line and rich singing throughout the whole range. The intonation of the chromatic notes needs to be well pitched over the typical Tchaikovskian harmonies underneath. The pianist should cut after the opening section to seven bars before the Andantino alla breve.

**125. Werther ... Werther ...**
   (Letter scene) (Charlotte)
Werther (1892), Act III fig 143
Massenet [6'20"] 📖 EP7553

*Frankfurt, c.1780: Charlotte has married Albert to please her dead mother, but is still in love with Werther. Charlotte, alone and missing her lover, muses on how often she re-reads his letters, and regrets that she sent him away until Christmas. Now, in his last letter, she reads with breathless anxiety that he is due back. If he should fail to appear, she would weep and tremble for him.*

This dramatic aria, full of contrasts, demands extraordinary emotional power. The section in which Charlotte reads the letters must be clearly portrayed, reserving a special colour for them. Keep the notes marked with stress marks long, and in the last section make sure that the long notes have no 'weight' but rather a feeling of emotional 'stretching' as if Charlotte has to summon up courage to read the final letter.

**126. Va! laisse couler mes larmes** (Charlotte)
Werther (1892), Act III fig 167
Massenet [2'] 📖 EP7553

*Frankfurt, c.1780: Sophie, Charlotte's younger sister, has arrived to find Charlotte emotionally upset over her lover Werther's letters. Sophie knows the reason and, when she mentions Werther's name, tears appear again in Charlotte's eyes. In the aria, Charlotte says that tears must be allowed to flow, otherwise they will return back into the body and beat against the heart and break it.*

This is a useful, short aria, which demonstrates intensity of love and emotional commitment.

**127. Acerba voluttà** (Principessa)
Adriana Lecouvreur (1902), Act II fig I
Cilea [4']

*Paris, 1730: The Princess of Bouillon is anxiously waiting for Maurizio in her secret hideout. She experiences a lover's jealousy and prays to the Star of the East to bring him to her.*

A very useful aria, because it is dramatic and yet not too heavy. The emotional agitation of waiting leads into a glorious prayer. It is best to underlay the last phrase like this: 'scor-' on the D, '-ta il' on the E♭, 'mio' on the E, 'a-' on the C as a crotchet, and finally '-mor' on the F. The text before figure 4, 'fra dubbiezza e disìo', uses a poetical form of the word 'desìo'.

**128. Sein wir wieder gut** (Komponist)
Ariadne auf Naxos (1912), Prologue fig 108
Richard Strauss [2'45"]

*Paris 18th century: Before the performance of their opera, the Music
Master has been trying to pacify all the temperamental personalities
involved in putting on an opera. In response to his address to the Composer
himself, the latter sings of how they are friends again and how he has learnt
that, although there are dark depths in the world and exquisite poetry,
music is the holiest art of all. Suddenly the buffi characters cross the stage
and the music becomes dissonant; the Composer reacts angrily, but the
Music Master reminds him that he allowed them to be part of the opera.
Yet the Composer is still furious, screaming at the Music Master for drag-
ging him into this crazy world: let him go hungry and die in his own
world.*

A wonderful, big, passionate aria requiring complete command of the
whole range. It is not to be undertaken lightly and must be musically
secure. It is best to finish at figure 117. This is one of the few roles in
opera where you are allowed to sound musical.

**129. Flowers bring to ev'ry year** (Lucretia)
(Recit: Give him this orchid)
The Rape of Lucretia (1946), Act II sc 2 fig 71
Britten [3'20"]

*Rome, 500 BC: Lucretia is in a mad state, having been raped by
Tarquinius in the night. She orders her maid, Lucia, to send an orchid to
Lucretia's husband Collatinus, expressing in her shame that only flowers are
chaste.*

A dramatic, violent, declamatory section needing strong singing, followed by an aria with a line lying in the middle of the voice. Make a
small cut of eight bars after the second bar of figure 74 to two bars
before figure 75.

# Contralto

**130. Ah! mon fils, sois béni** (Fidès)
Le prophète (1849), Act II no 10
Meyerbeer [3'50"] 📖 EP7553

*Holland, 1534–35: Fidès, mother of John of Leyden, has asked permission from the Lord of the Manor, Count Oberthal, for the marriage of Bertha to John, but the Count has taken a fancy to Bertha and takes her into his castle. In John's inn at Leyden, Bertha arrives, having escaped from the castle. The Count has followed and demands her return, using his mother as hostage. John relents, handing over Bertha, and Fidès sings this aria thanking John for saving her life and saying that he is blessed by God.*

A compact aria demonstrating legato singing, beautiful phrasing and good quality tone throughout the whole range.

**131. Condotta ell'era in ceppi** (Azucena)
Il trovatore (1853), Act II no 10
Verdi [5'15"]

*Biscay, 15th century: Azucena, a gypsy from Biscay, saw her mother burnt at the stake by the Count di Luna's father, after her mother was discovered by the cradle of the Count's brother. Azucena swore revenge and stole the child, in order to throw him on to the fire. But, in her terrible state, she threw instead her own son. She has brought up the Count's brother, Manrico, with the purpose of making him the instrument of her revenge. In this aria she continues to recount the whole horrific story to Manrico.*

This big, dramatic aria is a narration with interjections from Manrico. There is opportunity for demonstrating a wide range of colours, and observation of Verdi's varied phrasing marks will add to the excitement of Azucena's dramatic story-telling.

**132. Re dell'abisso, affrettati**
(Mme Arvidson/Ulrica)
Un ballo in maschera (1859), Act I sc 2 fig 38
Verdi [4'15" with short intro.]

*Sweden, 1792: Mme Arvidson (Ulrica) is preparing for her fortune telling. She first calls the King of the Underworld, hearing the thrice-sounded call of the owl and the salamander, and then the answer from the grave. In the second section, she announces the arrival of the King of the Underworld who holds the key to the future. The crowd cries out triumphantly and she silences them.*

A good audition aria for a heavy voice, requiring tremendous power and stamina. After the end of the first section, cut to twelve bars before 'È lui!'. The triplets that occur throughout the piece should be sung with a forward energy, and the breathing in the final climax of the second section must be carefully managed.

**133. Weiche, Wotan** (Erda)
Das Rheingold (1869), sc 4 fig 71
Wagner [4']  📖 EP735

*Outside Valhalla, legendary: In order to release Freia, Goddess of Youth to the Gods, Wotan must pay the giants a ransom of a pile of gold matching her height. One chink is left unfilled and the giants demand the ring on Wotan's finger. Wotan knows the power of the ring and refuses to hand it over. Erda, Goddess of the Earth, rises out of the ground to warn Wotan about retaining the ring. She knows the past, present and future, and she can see the coming of the end of the Gods if he does not hand over the ring.*

This is a concise aria needing slow, expansive, rich singing. It does not show off the lower range as Erda's role does in *Siegfried*. It is best to end the aria with the words 'Sinn' in Sorg' and Furcht!'. Wagner suggested in the original rehearsals that the delivery of the lines should be slow and very expressive, giving the impression of Erda's spirit sinking back into itself like fading light.

**134. Voce di donna** (La Cieca)
La Gioconda (1876), Act I
Ponchielli [2'45"]

*Venice, 17th century: La Cieca, Gioconda's blind mother, has been manip-ulated into being arrested as a witch by Barnaba, an Inquisition spy. He*

loves Gioconda and hopes to force her mother to persuade her to love him.
At this point, the head of the Inquisition, Alvise, and his wife, Laura,
appear. Gioconda, with Laura's help, is successful in pleading for Cieca's
release. Cieca sings this aria, thanking Laura, whom she can only imagine
through her voice to be an angel. She offers her a rosary in recompense and
prays for blessings to come to her.

A short, expressive aria demonstrating good line. It should end with the
phrases sung above the ensemble.

**135. Se tu sapessi** (Frugola)
Il tabarro (1918), fig 32 to 40
Puccini [2']

*Paris, early-20th century: Frugola, married to a stevedore, talks to
Giorgetta, wife of Michele, the owner of a barge. Frugola shows off all the
oddments in her bag, which she has picked up from the streets. In the second verse she talks of her cat and its philosophy that it is better to be single
and comfortable, than romantic and to have your heart broken with grief.*

A character aria requiring good use of text and direct, raw singing.
Make a cut after the third bar of figure 35 to seven bars before
figure 37.

# Tenor arias

## Buffo tenor

**136. Frisch zum Kampfe!** (Pedrillo)
Die Entführung aus dem Serail (1782), Act II no 13
Mozart [3'10"]  EP4233

*Turkey, 16th century: Pedrillo has told Blonde of his plan to drug Osmin
and make an escape. In this aria he tries, in spite of his nerves, to stir up
the courage to deal with Osmin.*

A strong, four-square aria requiring contrast between hesitation and
decision and well-pronounced text. Be very clear about the three styles
of music (i.e. the beginning, at bar 12 and at bar 17) which Mozart
alternates with such skill. Allow the German text to have as much line
as possible so that the voice is never under pressure.

**137. To, to me vhlavě leží!** (Vašek)
Prodaná Nevěsta (The Bartered Bride)
(1866), Act III sc 1
Smetana [2'40"]

*Bohemia, 19th century: Kecal, a marriage broker, has persuaded Mařenka's parents to wed their daughter to Vašek, whom they do not know to be a shy, stammering lad. Mařenka talked to him without his knowing who she was, and informed him that Mařenka is a flighty girl, advising him to woo another girl like the one to whom he is talking. In this aria, he is mourning the disappearance of this pretty girl, and is worried about what his mother will say when she finds out that he has given up Mařenka.*

A simple character aria; it is very touching in its lamentation, which should not be overdone.

**138. Vainement, ma bien-aimée – Aubade** (Mylio)
(Recit: Puisqu'on ne peut fléchir)
Le roi d'Ys (1888), Act III fig 174
Lalo [3'15"]  EP7554

*Breton, legendary: Mylio is due to marry Rozenn and, in Breton custom, her room is protected by her bridesmaids. He sings this serenade to plead his cause.*

A light, two-verse aria which requires floating high A's and finesse of phrasing. Begin at 'Puisqu'on ne peut fléchir' and note that in the full score there is no *accelerando* before the aria begins.

**139. O Colombina – Serenata** (Beppe)
I pagliacci (1892), Act II
Leoncavallo [2']

*Calabria, 1865–70: Arlecchino, in the stage play, sings this serenade to Colombine, asking her to open her window and show her face.*

A very light aria, requiring delicate phrasing and a beautiful silvery tone.

# Lyric tenor

**140. O wie ängstlich** (Belmonte)
(Recit: Konstanze!)
Die Entführung aus dem Serail (1782), Act I no 4
Mozart [5'20"] 📖 EP736

*Turkey, 16th century: After hearing that his lover, Konstanze, has remained true, and as he has a boat waiting to help them escape, Belmonte sings of his love and his anxious waiting.*

A cantabile aria with long, melismatic passages contrasted with declamatory sections. Let the orchestra initiate the new ideas and the vocal phrases will become reactions to them. It is as if the singer needs to use the vocal line to 'explain' what the orchestra is portraying underneath, feeling the text often in one in a bar.

**141. Dalla sua pace** (Don Ottavio)
(Recit: Come mai creder deggio)
Don Giovanni (Vienna 1788), Act I no 11
Mozart [4'20"] 📖 EP736

*Seville, 17th century: After telling how he will honour Donna Anna's wish for vengeance on Don Giovanni, Don Ottavio muses on the fact that, whatever she suffers, he will suffer it likewise.*

An aria lying often around high G with a very slow line which is hard to sustain. It is important to communicate its strong feeling of nobility in the phrasing. Do this by allowing the sentences to begin with long upbeats, which will become apparent from pronunciation of the Italian text.

**142. Il mio tesoro intanto** (Don Ottavio)
Don Giovanni (1787), Act II no 22
Mozart [4'15"] 📖 EP4233

*Seville, 17th century: Don Ottavio, after promising Zerlina, Masetto and Elvira that he will contact the law and have Don Giovanni arrested, asks*

*them to go to Donna Anna and console her by telling her that he is
seeking vengeance.*

An aria lying, like 'Dalla sua pace', around high G, it is hard to make
interesting. There should be a feeling of one in a bar, though the
orchestra supports the vocal line in two in a bar. The runs need careful
phrasing and well-intonated chromatic notes.

**143. Un'aura amorosa** (Ferrando)
Così fan tutte (1790), Act I no 17
Mozart [3'30"]    📖 EP4233, EP736, EP8902

*Naples, 18th century: Ferrando sings of his love, comparing it to a gentle
breeze, which sweetly restores life to his spirit.*

A cantabile aria requiring beautiful tone and superb phrasing, especially
in the melismas. In Mozart's day an appoggiatura before two notes of
the same pitch was sounded as only two notes, the first thus becoming
the appoggiatura note. This applies to the phrase 'bisogno non ha'.
Shape the final phrase as a hemiola – Ferrando is still old-fashioned,
witness the orchestral playout.

**144. Dies Bildniss ist bezaubernd schön** (Tamino)
Die Zauberflöte (1791), Act I no 3
Mozart [3'35"]    📖 EP4233, EP736, EP8902

*Egypt, legendary: Tamino has just been given the portrait of Pamina by the
Queen of the Night's three ladies. He falls in love with Pamina, as was
magically planned by the Queen.*

This is an aria which demands exquisite phrasing and beautiful line.
The ending is hard to manage and needs careful breathing. The impression should be of a dialogue between Tamino and his inner thoughts,
represented by the orchestra. He is slowly discovering for the first time
what love is.

**145. Languir per una bella** (Lindoro)
(Cabaletta: Contenta quest'alma)
L'italiana in Algeri (1813), Act I no 2
Rossini [2' + 3'35"]

*Algiers, 18th century: Lindoro, who is the favourite slave of the Bey of Algiers, longs for his loved one far away – Isabella.*

This high coloratura aria contains a cavatina and a cabaletta. The shaping of the melismas should be smoothly executed as if they were longing sighs or declarations of his constant love. The pianist obviously needs to shorten the introduction.

**146. Ecco ridente in cielo** (Almaviva)
Il barbiere di Siviglia (1816), Act I no 1
Rossini [3'20" with short intro.] EP4233

*Seville, 17th century: Count Almaviva, accompanied by Fiorello's band, sings this serenade up to Rosina's balcony. He pleads for her to appear, and imagines what the moment will be like when he sees her.*

A lyrical, florid aria requiring ecstatic feeling and tasteful, well-shaped ornamentation. A cut may be made from figure 25 to figure 26. The pianist should note that the orchestration of the first section is little more than a guitar pizzicato with some sustained chords in the strings. In the sixth bar after figure 23 there are no semiquavers in the second half of the bar. (See Ricci, *Book of Cadenzas*.)

**147. Una furtiva lagrima** (Nemorino)
L'elisir d'amore (1832), Act II sc 8 fig 67
Donizetti [3'45"] EP4233, EP736

*Italy, 19th century: Nemorino, a simple peasant, in love with Adina, has a rival, Belcore, a sergeant. Nemorino has been buying elixirs of love from a local quack, and he has paid for the last one by agreeing to enlist in the army. Now he is admired by all the village girls, because the death of a rich uncle has made him suddenly rich and attractive. He sings that he wishes only that his love will be returned by Adina.*

A beautiful audition aria demanding absolute bel canto. The opening phrase is renowned because of the difficulty of singing the first word with good tone. The crescendos on the dotted minims must be carefully managed so that the beauty of voice is not distorted.

**148. Pour mon âme** (Tonio)
La fille du régiment (1840), Act I fig 75
Donizetti [4']

*Swiss Tyrol, 1815: Tonio has loved the 'mascot' of the regiment, Marie, ever since she fell off a cliff into his arms. He has joined her regiment to be always near her, and now confesses to the soldiers that he loves her. In this section, the soldiers, acting as Marie's guardians, allow him to marry her, and he sings of his luck in becoming a military husband.*

A bravura waltz-aria showing off high C's – eight in all with perhaps an optional extra one in the last phrase.

**149. Spirto gentil** (Fernando)
La favorita (La favorite) (1840), Act IV fig 17
Donizetti [2'30"]  📖 EP7554

*Spain, c.1340: Fernando married Leonora, not knowing that she was the mistress of King Alfonso XI of Castile. He failed to receive a letter in which she attempted to tell him the truth, and the superior of the Monastery of St James, where Fernando was once a novice, is the first person to tell him the whole story. Fernando recants his marriage vows and re-enters the monastery. In this aria he remembers his love, but prays that the false hope for it will flee from his heart: Leonora caused him to forget his father's grief and his country.*

A short, high aria, which is very useful for auditions. All the phrases tend to shape themselves around the middle of the bar and it is thus important to sing through the barlines. The original language is French.

### 150. Ach! so fromm, ach so traut –
### M'appari tutt'amor (Lionel)
Martha (1847), Act III no 15
Flotow [2'50"] 📖 EP736, EP4233

*Richmond, c.1710: Lionel, who is foster-brother to a farmer called Plunkett, having been left as a child on the doorstep of Plunkett's father, is in love with Martha. She is really Lady Harriet, maid of honour to Queen Anne, and is curing her boredom by going around in disguise. In her travels she and her maid, Nancy, have deliberately allowed themselves to be hired as servants to Lionel and Plunkett. When the girls arrive at the farmer's house, an aged cousin rescues them. Lionel is sad at her disappearance and sings this aria describing her beauty.*

A simple, cantabile aria often sung in Italian. It lies awkwardly around F and G and so requires good control over the break in the voice.

### 151. Horch, die Lerche singt im Hain (Fenton)
Die lustigen Weiber von Windsor (1849),
   Act II no 7B
Nicolai [4'] 📖 EP736, EP4233

*Windsor, c.1400: Fenton, among other serenaders unbeknown to him, comes to serenade Anne in Mr Page's garden. The serenade has a standard text asking her to open her window and hear the lark. Whoever is in love will understand its call.*

A short, two-verse aria demonstrating line and beauty of tone but with only a small range.

### 152. De' miei bollenti spiriti (Alfredo)
(Recit: Lunge da lei)
La traviata (1853), Act II
Verdi [3'5"]

*Near Paris, 1850: Violetta, a courtesan, has left the pleasures of Paris to live in the country with Alfredo. He sings of the joy he has found since they moved there three months ago, and that they are both happy. He remem-*

*bers the day when she said she wished to be his love, and since then he has been in heaven.*

A short aria with recitative, demonstrating energy and vivacity of voice. The recitative should keep a sense of lyrical longing in spite of the busy orchestral introduction. Make sure the final 'vivo' is on C♮ and D (not C♯ and D). This is a hard aria to accompany, as room must be given to the singer while maintaining the agitated excitement of the semiquavers.

**153. Ô Paradis** (Vasco de Gama)
L'Africaine (1865), Act IV no 15
Meyerbeer [2'40"] 📖 EP7554

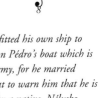

*East coast of Africa, early-16th century: Vasco has fitted his own ship to explore the coast of Africa and has met up with Don Pédro's boat which is leading an official expedition. Don Pédro is his enemy, for he married Vasco's love, Inès, and yet Vasco still boards his boat to warn him that he is off course. This information was incorrectly given by a native, Nélusko, who loves a native girl, Sélika, who in turn loves Vasco. Don Pédro has Vasco bound, but then a storm wrecks them on a reef, and Nélusko signals the natives to massacre them. Vasco escapes, and finds himself in a tropical paradise of which he sings. He sees a Hindu temple, and realizes that this is the land for which he has been searching for many years.*

A high, cantabile aria full of gorgeous phrases. Begin at 'Pays merveilleux' and sing only the cavatina. The French text must be pronounced broadly, to give the aria a feeling of expansiveness.

**154. Ah, lève-toi, soleil!** (Roméo)
(Recit: L'amour!)
Roméo et Juliette (1867), Act II no 7
Gounod [4'15"] 📖 EP7554

*Verona, 14th century: Romeo, before Juliet's balcony, suddenly becomes aware of her through her window. He compares her to the sun which rises and causes all the other stars to fade away.*

A fairly high aria with big phrases, it requires very secure high B♭'s. These phrases are quite short, creating the effect of Romeo's anticipatory excitement.

**155. Kuda, kuda** (Lenski)

Eugene Onegin (1879), Act II sc 2 no 17

Tchaikovsky [5'30"]  EP7582

*Russia, late-18th century: Lenski has challenged Onegin to a duel, after Onegin flirted with his love, Olga. Onegin is late, and as Lenski awaits his arrival in the early morning, he sings nostalgically and poetically of his youth and how he must meet his fate. Only the memory of Olga gives him hope.*

An aria with wonderful, sweeping phrases which lies generally in the middle of the voice. In the accompaniment, 14 bars before the end, the harmony should include C♮'s in the middle of the bar.

**156. En fermant les yeux – Le rêve** (Des Grieux)

Manon (1884), Act II fig 133

Massenet [2'15"]  EP7554

*Paris, 1721: Des Grieux has just posted a letter to his father telling him that he proposes to marry Manon. On returning home, Des Grieux finds Manon crying. He tells her how he was lost in dreaming on his way home. In this dream he saw a house in a garden with flowers and birds, but it still was not heaven without his love, Manon.*

An aria requiring tender and legato singing. It lies generally in the middle of the voice.

**157. Ah! fuyez, douce image** (Des Grieux)

(Recit: Je suis seul!)

Manon (1884), Act III sc 2 fig 246

Massenet [4']  EP7554

*Paris, 1721: Des Grieux has now entered holy orders after he was taken away from Manon by his father. His father arrives at the Seminary of St*

*Sulpice to persuade him to renounce his vocation and marry a suitable girl.*
*He refuses and, after his father leaves, prays that God will exorcise the*
*image of Manon from his mind and leave him in peace.*

A recitative followed by two verses of the aria, linked by another recitative. This is a big, dramatic aria requiring much emotional strength. Make sure that the double dots are observed and sung with passion, without losing tone on the semiquaver each time.

**158. Pourquoi me réveiller** (Werther)
   Werther (1892), Act III fig 190
   Massenet [2'25"] 📖 EP7554

*Frankfurt, 1780: Against his stronger instincts, Werther has returned on*
*the appointed day to his love, Charlotte, who is married to Albert. Now*
*they find themselves browsing in some books, which revive strong memories.*
*Charlotte finds some poems of Ossian and they remind him of how he used*
*to translate them. In the aria he sings the poem: 'Why did you awaken me,*
*O Spring, for the hour of storms and sadness is close at hand. The traveller*
*in the valley will remember my former glory and he will search for it, but*
*will find only sorrow and misery.'*

A cantabile, two-verse aria demonstrating wonderful line and phrasing. Massenet's phrasing is clearly marked, and observing it will convey Werther's inspired spontaneous translation of the original Scottish of the poem.

**159. Dal labbro il canto estasiato vola** (Fenton)
   Falstaff (1893), Act III sc 2 fig 23
   Verdi [2'15" with short intro.]

*Windsor, c.1400: Fenton, dressed for his part in the masquerade to frighten*
*Falstaff by Herne's oak at midnight, sings in the night air a song of love.*
*The wood seems to respond, and soon he hears his love Nannetta reply.*

A short aria demonstrating cantabile phrases and movement over the break of the voice. You will need to find a way to end the aria satisfactorily, perhaps by finishing after the phrase 'Bocca baciata non

perde ventura', with the pianist using Nannetta's phrase to end the
music in a cadence.

**160. Heaven helps those who help themselves** (Albert)
Albert Herring (1947), Act II sc 2 fig 85 to 95
Britten [3'30"]

*Lexford, East Suffolk, May 1900: Albert has been chosen as May King as
there seems to be no local girl well-behaved enough to be the Queen. He
works in his mother's green-grocery shop and is often teased by Sid, a butch-
er's hand, because he does not go out with the girls. At the May celebra-
tions, Sid laced Albert's drink with rum, which caused an embarrassing
bout of hiccups and upset the formality of the occasion. That evening,
Albert overhears Sid and his girlfriend, Nancy, making a loving assignation
for that night. Albert suddenly becomes bitter against the world, which
seems to laugh at his simplicity, calling him 'Albert the Good!'. Now is the
time to decide whether or not to change all that.*

A passionate aria which has different sections that show off many
Britten characteristics – use of coloratura, portamentos and clear declamation. Britten always marks his scores with great precision, and these
markings should be well observed and integrated into the character of
your singing.

**161. Love, too frequently betrayed** (Tom Rakewell)
The Rake's Progress (1951), Act I sc 2 fig 151
Stravinsky [2'45"]

*London, 18th century: Tom Rakewell has been taken by Nick Shadow to a
brothel in London. In order to be initiated, he must answer some questions
and sing a song. He sings to Love, who is so often forgotten or avoided, asking that Love should not forget him in case, in dying, he cannot call on
Love's name.*

An aria with a small range but containing long phrases demonstrating
breath control and beautiful tone.

# Italian tenor

## 162. **Fra poco a me ricovero** (Edgardo)
    (Recit: Tombe degli avi miei)
    (Cabaletta: Tu che a Dio spiegasti l'ali)
    Lucia di Lammermoor (1835), Act III sc 2
    Donizetti [4'30" with short intro. + 2'10"]   EP4233

*Scotland, 1700: Edgardo waits by his forefathers' tomb for the arrival of Lucia's brother Enrico; they are to fight a duel in which Edgardo intends to let himself be killed. In the aria's first part he sings of his sadness, in contrast with his mental image of Lucia in her married happiness with Arturo. Edgardo hopes she will still remember him. On meeting some mourners and hearing of Lucia's death, he prays in the cabaletta to be reunited with Lucia in heaven.*

An emotional recitative followed by a slow, high line, centred around high F♯ and G. The cabaletta probably does not need to be sung because it also comprises a similarly slow high line. The whole scene is often transposed down a semitone in performance. If you sing the cabaletta, cut straight to the introduction. (See Ricci, *Book of Cadenzas*.)

## 163. **Quando le sere al placido** (Rodolfo)
    (Recit: Oh! fede negar potessi)
    Luisa Miller (1849), Act II Finale fig 37
    Verdi [4'50"]

*Tyrol, first half of 18th century: Rodolfo, the son of Count Walter, has fallen in love with Luisa, daughter of an old soldier. Unfortunately the machinations of Wurm, who loves Luisa, and the Duchess Federica, who loves Rodolfo, have led to Luisa's father being imprisoned. Luisa is forced to write a letter saying that she never loved Rodolfo. It is arranged that the letter will fall into Rodolfo's hands, and he sings this aria, realizing she was untrue to him. He remembers the time when they walked hand in hand on a quiet evening – now she has betrayed him.*

A strong recitative followed by a passionate, cantabile aria. Try to follow Verdi's phrasing exactly – legato phrase-marks, staccatos with a phrase-mark (this indicates more intention in the words but they are still to be sung legato), and normal staccatos which denote declamation.

**164. Questa o quella** (Il Duca)
Rigoletto (1851), Act I
Verdi [2'] 📖 EP4248

*Mantua, 16th century: The Duke of Mantua shows off to a courtier, Borsa, how he desires Ceprano's wife. He loves all women: it could be this girl one day, that girl the next. He detests faithfulness and will defy all jealous husbands to achieve his conquests.*

An elegant aria requiring a good top to the voice and clear diction. A cadenza can be added at the end of the second verse. (See Ricci, *Book of Cadenzas.*)

**165. Parmi veder le lagrime** (Il Duca)
(Recit: Ella mi fu rapita!)
Rigoletto (1851), Act II
Verdi [5']

*Mantua, 16th century: The Duke of Mantua loves Gilda, at whose house he was disturbed. When he returned, she was missing. Back at his palace, he muses on the shock of her disappearance and swears vengeance on the perpetrators. Gilda has awakened in him for the first time the flame of constant love. In the aria, he imagines her face at the moment when he told her that his name was Gualtier Maldè. The angels must help her, for she is as beautiful as any angel.*

A good audition aria with a recitative full of contrasts and a high-ranging cantabile section. It is good to sing the high ossia B♭ –G♭ –D♭ on the last 'agl'angeli' and you can omit the semiquaver melisma in the final cadenza. Notice the use of both smorzatura accents, denoting *sforzando*, and tenuto accents. It is probably best to leave out the cabaletta.

**166. La donna è mobile** (Il Duca)
Rigoletto (1851), Act III
Verdi [2'10"]

*Mantua, 16th century: Rigoletto has hired Sparafucile, an assassin, to kill the Duke. Sparafucile's sister, Maddalena, has enticed the Duke to visit a solitary inn where, watched in secret by Rigoletto and his daughter Gilda, he arrives disguised as a soldier and asks for a room and wine. This aria is about the fickleness of women, who change their affections like a feather in the wind. Whoever trusts them is sure to be unhappy.*

A well-known, two-verse aria demanding flexibility of voice and good phrasing. A cadenza can be added at the end of the second verse. (See Ricci, *Book of Cadenzas*.)

**167. Salut! demeure chaste et pure** (Faust)
(Recit: Quel trouble inconnu)
Faust (1859), Act III no 8
Gounod [5'10"]  📖 EP7554, EP4233

*Germany, 16th century: Faust is brought by Mephistopheles into Marguerite's garden and he muses on the magic atmosphere of her dwelling place.*

This contains a short recitative, which is followed by a cavatina with a slow line. It needs a safe high C and excellent pacing to prepare the ending. All the phrases need to begin with the feeling of an upbeat, in order to communicate all Faust's longing.

**168. Ah, la paterna mano** (Macduff)
(Recit: O figli, o figli miei!)
Macbeth (1847/1865), Act IV sc 1 no 18
Verdi [3'30"]  📖 EP4248

*Scotland, 1040: Macduff is leading a group of refugees on the borders of Scotland. He tells of his slaughtered children and blames it all on himself, praying that he will meet the tyrant Macbeth face to face. But if Macbeth escapes, may he be forgiven.*

A good audition aria, concise with a short recitative. Like 'De' miei bollenti spiriti' from *La traviata* (No. 152), it lies mostly in the same area of the voice, so that the phrases need to be well shaped.

**169. Cielo! e mar!** (Enzo)
La Gioconda (1876), Act II
Ponchielli [3'45"]

*Venice, 17th century: Enzo is in love with Laura, wife of a head of the Inquisition, Alvise. Barnaba, a spy, has arranged an assignation for them on a fishing boat. As Enzo waits on the boat, he sings this aria describing the sky and the sea, and wonders from what heights or depths his angel will appear. His heart becomes excited, and he calls for her.*

A big, two-verse aria, demanding a good command of range and a rich voice. The phrases must always sound as if they are climbing to the heights, thus becoming very exciting. One can end with an optional high B♭.

**170. Donna non vidi mai** (Des Grieux)
Manon Lescaut (1893), Act I fig 33
Puccini [2']

*Amiens, second half of 18th century: In a courtyard of a coaching inn, Des Grieux has declared his love for Manon, who is on her way to a convent. They agree to meet again in a short while and, when she leaves, he sings this aria about her wonderful beauty, which he has never seen before. He repeats her name with ecstasy.*

This is a short aria with rich lines, generally lying quite high. Let the melody shape itself around each of the top notes in each phrase.

**171. Che gelida manina** (Rodolfo)
La bohème (1896), Act I fig 30
Puccini [4'15"]

*Paris, 1830: Mimì, Rodolfo's neighbour, has lost her key and now both of their candles have been blown out. Though Rodolfo has found the key,*

*he still pretends to be looking for it. As he touches her hand, he begins to poetise his feelings for her. He tells her who he is and how he makes a living as a poet. Her eyes have stolen all his secrets from him, and he asks her who she is.*

This is a very good audition aria, demonstrating a wide range, line and colours. It needs lots of charm and poetical fervour. You are naturally expected to sing the top C!

**172. Un dì all'azzurro spazio (Improvviso)**
    (Andrea Chénier)
    Andrea Chénier (1896), Act I fig 34
    Giordano [4'30"]

*Paris, French Revolution: Just before the Revolution, Chénier, a patriotic poet, is at a Château party. He is provokingly asked by Maddalena to improvise a poem, and he speaks of his love of the beautiful countryside, yet bemoans the dichotomy between the poor and those in authority in the towns. He turns to Maddalena and tells her not to scorn life for she knows nothing of love.*

An aria demanding good use of colour and a feel for the Italian line. The many repeated notes within the phrases should be used for clear declamation and for creating a sense of spontaneity and inspiration in Chénier's performance.

**173. Come un bel dì di maggio** (Andrea Chénier)
    Andrea Chénier (1896), Act IV fig 1
    Giordano [2'45"]

*Paris, French Revolution: Chénier and Gérard are both in love with the same woman, Maddalena. After a duel between them, Gérard allowed Chénier to escape but he is forced to sign an indictment against him by a spy of the Revolution. Chénier is arrested and is now in prison. He sings the verses he has just written about the end of his life, and offers up his soul to the Muses, asking for one final inspiration.*

A short, full aria requiring rich and passionate singing. The small ornaments should be well sung, keeping them within the melodic line.

**174. È la solita storia del pastore –**
     **Lamento di Federico** (Federico)
     L'arlesiana (1897), Act II fig 15
     Cilea [4']

*Provence, legendary: Federico has discovered that his lover from Arles is a*
*strumpet, that she has been with another man and that she has left his*
*mother's home. Baldassare, an old shepherd, and L'innocente, Federico's*
*own retarded brother, find Federico, and the shepherd tries to persuade him*
*to return. L'innocente is falling asleep as he repeats a line from the shep-*
*herd's story which has just been told. In this aria, Federico envies his broth-*
*er's sleep and wishes that he could sleep in oblivion. His peace has been*
*taken away, and he is suffering from the fatal vision of his love before him.*

A beautiful, concise, cantabile aria demonstrating command of
Italian line.

**175. L'anima ho stanca** (Maurizio)
     Adriana Lecouvreur (1902), Act II fig 15
     Cilea [1'25"]

*Paris, 1730: Maurizio tries to explain to the jealous Princess of Bouillon that,*
*even if his love for her has ceased, his memory of her will always remain.*

This is a very short aria, which is extremely useful in demonstrating
legato singing and varied colours.

**176. Hai ben ragione** (Luigi)
     Il tabarro (1918), Fig 44
     Puccini [2'30"]

*Paris, early-20th century: Luigi, a stevedore, is having an affair with*
*Giorgetta, wife of Michele who owns the barge. One of the other stevedores*
*says that drinking is his only pleasure. Luigi agrees, and bitterly sings that*
*they must suffer all the anguish of a worker's lot, and yield to the fate of*
*being crushed by their employers.*

A concise, strong aria, which requires good, direct singing.

# Youthful heroic tenor

**177. Se all'impero, amici Dei!** (Tito)
La clemenza di Tito (1791), Act II no 20
Mozart [4'45"]

*Rome, AD 79–81: Tito, the Roman Emperor, has sat in judgement on his best friend Sesto, who has been found guilty of a conspiracy against Tito's life. Tito tears up the death sentence and asks the gods to give him another heart in exchange for the imperial one he has, which is laden with a responsibility to be severe.*

A strong, four-square aria full of good runs, with a cantabile section in the middle.

**178. Durch die Wälder** (Max)
(Recit: Nein! länger trag'ich nicht die Qualen)
Der Freischütz (1821), Act I no 3
Weber [6'45"] 📖 EP736

*Bohemia, 17th century: Max, a forester, has lost another shooting match, defeated by a mere peasant, Kilian. He is teased and mocked, for he hopes to win Agathe, daughter of the head-ranger, at the prize shooting tomorrow. He is left alone and, in this aria, wonders why bad luck stays with him. In the first lyrical section, he remembers how he could shoot down any bird and bring it home to the welcoming smile of Agathe. Zamiel, a man of evil, hovers in the background hearing him recount the bad turn of events. In the second lyrical section, Max imagines Agathe waiting at her window for his next triumph. In the Allegro, he asks what darkness surrounds him, and wonders if God still exists.*

This scene comprises a recitative, moderato, recitative, Andante con moto, and an Allegro con fuoco. It contains many contrasts, lyrical and dramatic, and thus there is probably no need for another aria to complement it at an audition. It is a very effective piece using many different styles.

**179. Willst jenes Tag's du nicht dich mehr entsinnen** (Erik)

Der fliegende Holländer (1843),
Act III no 9A (or 8A)

Wagner [2'45"]

*Norway, 18th century: Erik has discovered that Senta's fascination for the Flying Dutchman in the legend has now been transferred to a stranger who has been led there in his boat by Daland, her father. She plans to be betrothed to this man. Erik tries to remind her of the past, for she was entrusted to his care by her father when the latter had to sail away. Did she not say she loved him and did he not feel it in her warmth towards him?*

This is a short cantabile aria, very useful for showing command of German line. It has, surprisingly, a very Italian shape and is best approached as if it were an Italian aria, with fluid shaping and all the turns well sung.

**180. Mein lieber Schwan!** (Lohengrin)

Lohengrin (1850), Act III sc 2 fig 74

Wagner [4'20"] 📖 EP736

*Brabant (Antwerp), first half of 10th century: Lohengrin, a mysterious unknown knight is the defender of Elsa against the accusations of Friedrich Telramund and Ortrud that she murdered her brother to gain the dukedom of Brabant. Lohengrin married Elsa on condition that she did not question his name or country, but the seeds of doubt flowered in Elsa's mind and, in the end, she asked those questions and the vow was broken. In the previous scene Lohengrin revealed his identity: he is a knight of the Holy Grail. The swan appears to take him home and, in this aria, he addresses it, telling it that the vow has lasted a year and that the swan would have been transformed. (Eventually, the swan is transformed into Elsa's brother, Godfrey.) Lohengrin then turns to Elsa, expressing his grief that the vow has been broken. He offers his horn, sword and ring to Godfrey, should he return, and bids Elsa a passionate farewell.*

This is a high role, and the aria demonstrates a lyrical melody, and declamatory and dramatic power. The pulse of the text should always be noted – often two or even one to a bar.

**181.** **Oh, tu che in seno agl'angeli** (Don Alvaro)
(Recit: Della natal sua terra)
La forza del destino (1862), Act III no 16
Verdi [3'45"]

*Italy, 18th century: Don Alvaro, fleeing from the accidental death of his lover's father, has enlisted in the Spanish army fighting in Italy. In the recitative he sings the story of his life – born in prison, educated in the desert, ignorant of his royal blood. He prays to Leonora, whom he imagines among the angels, to look down on him with pity and allow him to die.*

An extremely difficult aria with a wide range with many high A♭'s extending to B♭, which should be tackled only by a 'tenore superbo'. Begin the recitative at 'Della natal sua terra'.

**182.** **Celeste Aida** (Radames)
(Recit: Se quel guerrier)
Aida (1871), Act I
Verdi [4'15"]

*Memphis, Reign of the Pharaohs: The priests are making sacrifices to Isis to discover who should lead the army against the Ethiopians. Radames hopes to be the chosen one, so that he may return in glory to his love Aida, who is a slave in Princess Amneris's court. He describes Aida's beauty and imagines her adorned with regal crown enthroned next to the sun.*

A very difficult recitative and aria with climbing phrases and difficult high B♭'s. It requires good line in the voice and wonderful breath control.

**183.** **La fleur que tu m'avais jetée** (Don José)
Carmen (1875), Act II no 17
Bizet [3'45"]

*Seville, 1820: Don José has just spent two months in prison for letting Carmen escape. He comes to visit her in the tavern, but the bugle has sounded for the soldiers to return to their barracks. She taunts him about going back, saying that he does not love her anymore. He replies that he*

will prove his love. In the aria, he sings that he kept in prison the flower she threw to him when he first saw her, and that he could never forget her.

A good concise aria, showing off range of voice and beautiful phrasing. The text has a feeling of one in a bar and very often the word on the first beat is not the most important word in the sentence. There must be an element of narration in which Don José proves his love for Carmen. One should avoid the pitfall of the tenor 'piangendo' tone. The final high B♭ would have originally been sung in falsetto, and this takes courage; but take care that it is not loud.

**184. Vesti la giubba** (Canio)
(Recit: Recitar!)
I pagliacci (1892), Act I end
Leoncavallo [2'45"]

*Calabria, 1865–70: Canio has overheard his wife, Nedda, declaring her love to a stranger, Silvio, and must now prepare himself for his performance as Pagliaccio. He owes it to his public to find a way to transform all his grief into buffoonery and grimaces.*

This is a short aria which demands extreme emotional singing and a full, expansive tone. Remember that it is marked *con dolore* and not *piangendo*.

**185. Recondita armonia** (Cavaradossi)
Tosca (1900), Act I
Puccini [2'40"]

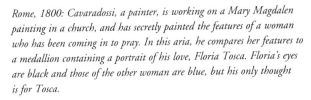

*Rome, 1800: Cavaradossi, a painter, is working on a Mary Magdalen painting in a church, and has secretly painted the features of a woman who has been coming in to pray. In this aria, he compares her features to a medallion containing a portrait of his love, Floria Tosca. Floria's eyes are black and those of the other woman are blue, but his only thought is for Tosca.*

A good, concise aria calling for good line and full singing. In the middle section, 'L'arte nel suo mistero', the text should be beautifully intonated on the B♭'s and A's.

**186. E lucevan le stelle** (Cavaradossi)
Tosca (1900), Act III
Puccini [2'20"]

*Rome, 1800: Cavaradossi, in his prison cell awaiting the dawn and his execution, muses on the stars and remembers a meeting in the garden with Tosca, his love. He realizes that he will die at a time when he has never loved life so much.*

A short aria, full of wonderful phrases and an opening declamatory passage, in which the Italian narration should be eloquently fluid.

**187. Ch'ella mi creda** (Johnson)
La fanciulla del West (1910), Act III fig 26
Puccini [2'15"]

*California, 1849–50: Johnson, a bandit, is condemned to death on the gallows by the crowd, encouraged by the sheriff, Jack Rance, who wants his girl Minnie. Johnson is allowed a last word before his death, so he sings of his love, thus annoying Jack Rance even more.*

This very slow, concise aria requires incredible richness of voice and intensity of expression. The portamentos should be full of passion.

**188. Nessun dorma** (Calaf)
Turandot (1926), Act III sc 1 fig 4
Puccini [2'35"]

*Far East, antiquity: Calaf has answered the three riddles, but has set one riddle for Turandot to solve before sunrise: to find out his name. The whole city cannot sleep, while Turandot's soldiers scourge the town to discover the answer. Calaf sings of his impending victory.*

A rich aria with a solid line demanding a good high B at the end.

# Heroic tenor

**189. Gott! welch Dunkel hier!** (Florestan)
(Aria: In des Lebens Frühlingstagen)
Fidelio (1805), Act II no 11
Beethoven [6'10"] 📖 EP4233

*Seville, 18th century: Florestan describes the conditions in the prison and,
in the cavatina, finds comfort that he has done his duty. Then he sees a
vision of Leonore, his wife, who seems to lead him to freedom.*

A recitative with long, demanding lines, and a sustained cavatina. The
cabaletta requires great stamina and technique, especially in its final lines
with their difficult text. These last phrases need careful technical working-
out like the end of Tamino's 'Dies Bildniss' (No. 144), with their slowly
climbing notes – F, F♯, G, A, B♭ and the following B♭ arpeggio. Notice that
the appoggiatura at the end of the phrase 'Wahrheit wagt'ich kühn zu
sagen' in the Adagio should be sung as just two notes, E♭ and D, as was the
convention in Beethoven's day. The pianist should play two to six bars of
introduction and shorten the playout.

**190. Winterstürme** (Siegmund)
Die Walküre (1870), Act I sc 3 fig 55B
Wagner [3'30"] 📖 EP736

*Hunding's hut, legendary: Siegmund, escaping from his enemies, finds him-
self in Hunding's hut, and discovers that Hunding is the chief of these same
enemies. He is allowed to remain as a guest for the night. Hunding's wife,
Sieglinde, feels a natural sympathy towards Siegmund who, unbeknown to
them both, is her brother. In this aria, the door has suddenly blown open
and the moon shines on them both, causing Siegmund to sing how spring
has arrived, gently sending the winter storms away. Spring was lured by its
own sister, Love, who lies deep within their beings.*

As in most Wagnerian roles, the middle and lower range are important,
and the aria also demonstrates melodic and declamatory singing. The text
of the third phrase should be 'Auf linden Lüften, leicht und lieblich'.

Be careful that in the phrase 'Zu seiner Schwester schwang er sich her' there is a glottal on 'er' to avoid its sounding like 'schwanger' (pregnant).

## 191. Dio! mi potevi scagliar tutti i mali (Otello)

Otello (1887), Act III sc 3 letter N
Verdi [3'30"]

*Cyprus, end of 15th century: Othello has just caused his wife, Desdemona, to flee from his jealous, hysterical fury, which Iago had subtly sparked off through his insinuations that Cassio was in love with her. Othello reflects that, if God had stripped him of all his glory, he could have coped, but to strip him of his love is too much to bear. At the last moment, Iago announces Cassio's presence.*

A dramatic aria demanding command of parlando, cantabile, and declamatory and spirited singing. Finish at 'Oh gioia!' (the final chord, two bars before the Allegro mosso, should be on the fourth beat). There should be a kind of hypnotic atmosphere, suggested by the orchestra in the first section, and the singer can produce a mesmeric feeling on the recurring A♭'s.

# Baritone arias

## Lyric baritone

**192. Donne mie, la fate a tanti** (Guglielmo)
Così fan tutte (1790), Act II no 26
Mozart [3'10"] 📖 EP4234

*Naples, 18th century: Guglielmo cynically addresses all women, telling them that, although they have deceived him, he will always adore them.*

This aria is full of text, requiring good diction and fluent phrasing of the Italian. Though the orchestra's *moto perpetuo* has a pulse of two in a bar, the vocal line must be shaped in one in a bar. The structure of four verses and refrains followed by a coda should be clearly delineated.

**193. Ein Mädchen oder Weibchen** (Papageno)
Die Zauberflöte (1791), Act II no 20
Mozart [3' two verses] 📖 EP4234

*Egypt, legendary: Papageno, in Sarastro's temple, is given food and wine but, on playing his bells, he remembers what is missing – a little wife.*

Probably a better audition aria than Papageno's first aria, especially if the middle verse is omitted. In its strophic use of an old popular melody it is important to keep the text 'alive' in order to capture the panel's interest.

**194. Largo al factotum della città** (Figaro)
Il barbiere di Siviglia (1816), Act I no 2
Rossini [5'] 📖 EP737

*Seville, 17th century: Figaro, on his way to his barber's shop at dawn, sings this cynical monologue about what a wonderfully busy trade he has and how everyone is always demanding his many talents.*

A marvellous audition aria, requiring a wonderful top to the voice, elegant diction and good stamina. The Italian text must be allowed to retain its own natural shape within the 6/8 musical rhythm, and the 'la's' should be given some meaning so as not to sound as if the singer has forgotten the words! It is worth singing the introductory 'La ran la lera' entries, though in the opera they are sung offstage (thus providing a few warm-up phrases to help the nerves). This is a tour de force for the pianist. (See Ricci, *Book of Cadenzas*.)

**195. Come Paride vezzoso** (Belcore)
L'elisir d'amore (1832), Act I Cavatina fig 29
Donizetti [2'55"]

*Italy, 19th century: Belcore, a sergeant, arrives in a village and addresses the maidens, asking them to accept his heart as well as his flowers.*

A two-verse aria, requiring good flexibility and line. As Belcore gains confidence, so the coloratura becomes more frequent and more exciting. The third beat of the bar is often the most important in the phrasing of the music.

**196. Bella siccome un angelo** (Malatesta)
Don Pasquale (1843), Act I sc 1
Donizetti [2'40"] 📖 EP4234

*Rome, early-19th century: Dr Malatesta describes in glowing terms a woman he says is his sister (in a convent), encouraging Don Pasquale to*

*believe she will marry him. This is to distract Don Pasquale from his threatened disinheritance of his nephew, and Malatesta's friend, Ernesto, because Ernesto wishes to marry Norina. In fact, in the aria Malatesta describes the features of Norina herself.*

A short cavatina of two verses which requires beautiful lyric tone and word painting. A wide range is needed in the cadenza.

**197. Ah! pescator, affonda l'esca** (Barnaba)
La Gioconda (1876), Act II
Ponchielli [2'15"]

*Venice, 17th century: Barnaba, a spy for the Inquisition, has guessed that Laura, wife of one of the heads of the Inquisition, Alvise, is in love with Enzo. Barnaba has divulged his suspicions to Enzo, promising to arrange a secret assignation with Laura. He is being helpful because he is in love with La Gioconda and wants to prove to her that Enzo does not love her any more. In this scene, Barnaba, disguised as a fisherman, sings a ballad to the other fishermen. It tells of the fisherman lowering his bait and catching his victim in his net. In the declamatory passage, he whispers to Isèpo, his accomplice, to keep a look-out in preparation for the assignation.*

A lilting ballad, which lies quite high, and needs good flexibility and phrasing. The staccatos in the middle section denote that the text should be well declaimed, in contrast to the Venetian style of the beginning.

# Cavalier-baritone

**198. Vedrò, mentr'io sospiro** (Il Conte)
(Recit: Hai già vinta la causa!)
Le nozze di Figaro (1786), Act III no 17
Mozart [4'30"] 📖 EP737

*Seville, 18th century: The Count has overheard Susanna whispering to Figaro 'without a lawyer you have won the legal action'. This crucial sentence means that, through her charms, Susanna can persuade the Count to*

*Baritone arias*

*pay the money that Figaro owes Marcellina. Now the Count realizes what Susanna is up to and, arguing through all the facts, concludes that he will yet be victorious and have vengeance on his servant, Figaro. The old rivalry between Figaro and Count Almaviva is still fresh and alive.*

A good audition aria with a big range and an important recitative with difficult pacing. This aria is full of jealousy and anger, which must be kept within an aristocratic bearing. The triplet run at the end must be clearly sung, leading to a comfortable high F♯.

**199. Cruda, funesta smania** (Enrico)
(Cabaletta: La pietade in suo favore)
Lucia di Lammermoor (1835), Act I sc 1
Donizetti [1'50" + 1'30" one verse]

*Scotland, 1700: Normanno has been telling Enrico of his suspicions that Enrico's sister, Lucia, has been having secret meetings with Enrico's deadly enemy, Edgardo. Enrico expresses his fury and disdain and, after the cavatina, the chorus returns to confirm Normanno's suspicions. Enrico sings of revenge in the cabaletta.*

A strong aria requiring much controlled anger and hate in the voice, and use of strong, dotted rhythms. The top of the voice must be easy to manage. Cut straight from cavatina to cabaletta, singing only one verse, and then cut to the last five full bars of singing. (See Ricci, *Book of Cadenzas*.)

**200. Ah! per sempre io ti perdei** (Riccardo)
(Recit: Or dove fuggo io mai?)
I puritani (1835), Act I sc 5 no 2
Bellini [4'10"]

*Plymouth, English Civil War: Riccardo has just been asked by Elvira's father to give up Elvira, so that she can marry the man she loves, Arturo. Riccardo tells Bruno of his feelings and how he wandered, full of sadness at losing her.*

An aria requiring good line and flexibility, with some long phrases needing disciplined breathing. In the recitative, cut after 'or che rimane a me?' directly to the cavatina. (See Ricci, *Book of Cadenzas*.)

**201. O du mein holder Abendstern** (Wolfram)
(Recit: Wie Todesahnung)
Tannhäuser (1845), Act III sc 2 fig 135
Wagner [4'30"] 📖 EP737

*Wartburgner Eisenach, early-13th century: Wolfram von Eschenbach, a knight of Wartburg, is waiting with Elizabeth, who is hoping that her love, Tannhäuser, will be returning from Rome, where he has been to ask forgiveness for his sins. As the pilgrims pass through the valley and evening falls, Elizabeth returns disappointedly to the castle, asking to be left alone. Wolfram sings to his lyre of the twilight, which is like a foreboding of death. He compares the sight of Elizabeth climbing the hill to a soul escaping from the awful night, with the evening star, which guides our way. He asks the star to greet his secret love as she climbs, like an angel, to the castle.*

An aria with a low range, demanding marvellous line and control of slow singing.

**202. Di Provenza il mar** (Germont)
La traviata (1853), Act II no 10
Verdi [4'5"] 📖 EP4249

*Near Paris, 1850: Germont, Alfredo's father, has persuaded his son's lover, Violetta, to leave him, because of the scandal the affair has caused Germont's family. A letter from Violetta has just been handed to Alfredo telling of her decision and, as he reads it, Germont returns. Germont sings this aria to soften the shock, by singing of their home in Provence, where the sun shines on all, and how God brings peace to everyone. In the second verse, he tells how much he himself has suffered because of Alfredo's way of life, but now he has found him he hopes God will bring him back to the bosom of the family.*

A high, two-verse arietta demonstrating line and control of the top of the voice. It is possible to begin in the preceding Allegro, 'Mio figlio!'.

Make sure that all Verdi's phrase-marks are observed, including the legato upbeats. The appoggiaturas must be fully sung.

**203. Avant de quitter ces lieux** (Valentine)
(Recit: O sainte médaille)
Faust (1859), Act II no 4 (or Act I sc 2 no 6)
Gounod [3'40"] 📖 EP4234, EP7555

*Germany, 16th century: Valentine, who is about to go to war, has been given a medallion by his sister, Marguerite, to protect him from harm in battle. He prays that his sister will be safe during his absence, and that he will be a brave soldier.*

This is a useful audition aria which shows off the top of the voice. It needs good phrasing over the four-square accompaniment. It is best to end the recitative at 'Reste là sur mon cœur' and to cut to the four bars marked *moderato* before the cavatina. The original key is E♭ major. The aria was first written in English ('Even bravest heart may swell') for the London production in 1864, but it is now usually sung in French.

**204. O Nadir, tendre ami** (Zurga)
(Recit: L'orage s'est calmé)
Les pêcheurs de perles (1863), Act III no 11
Bizet [5'15" short intro.] 📖 EP7555

*Ceylon, antiquity: Zurga, King of the Fishermen, has discovered that his best friend, Nadir, who has been captured by a Brahmin priest, is in love with Zurga's secret love, Leïla, a priestess. At the beginning of this scene a storm abates, and Zurga's emotions are still in turmoil, as he laments the imminent end of his friendship with Nadir.*

A recitative followed by a strong sweeping aria, full of great expression. The pianist must allow the singer considerable flexibility so that the music can be exquisitely shaped.

**205. Vī mne pisali** (Onegin)
Eugene Onegin (1879), Act I sc 3 no 12
Tchaikovsky [5'10"] 📖 EP7583

*Russia, late-18th century: Tatyana has sent a letter to Onegin, expressing her love. He meets her in the garden and tells her, frankly and coldly, that married life is not for him, and that she will have no difficulty in finding another man.*

The tessitura of this aria tends to remain in the area around E♭, so the phrasing of the cantabile vocal line is very important. The eloquence of Onegin's singing belittles Tatyana even more.

**206. Questo amor, vergogna mia** (Frank)
Edgar (1889), Act I fig 21
Puccini [2'30"]

*Flanders, c.1300: Frank is in love with Tigrana, who was brought up by his father after being abandoned in the village. He soliloquizes on this love, which is hopeless and humiliates him. She only derides his love, and yet he continues to love her.*

A short, high, cantabile aria which demonstrates a good, legato line.

**207. Look! Through the port comes
the moonshine astray!** (Billy Budd)
Billy Budd (1951), Act IV sc 1
Britten [5'10"]

*HMS Indomitable, 1797: Billy Budd, a new recruit, has been condemned to death after striking the Master of Arms, Claggart, and killing him. Claggart had falsely accused him of insubordination and mutinous plans, and the blow was Billy's reaction. At dawn, he meditates before his execution, imagining the action about to take place.*

This aria has very slow lines, requiring incredible concentration and intensity of emotion.

# Character baritone

**208. Cortigiani, vil razza** (Rigoletto)
Rigoletto (1851), Act II
Verdi [3'50"] 📖 EP4249

*Mantua, 16th century: Rigoletto, the court jester, has discovered that his daughter, Gilda, has been kidnapped, and suspects the courtiers of the deed. He nonchalantly tries to ascertain the truth and then turns on them, announcing that he knows his daughter has been taken by them, which surprises the court who believed Gilda was his girlfriend. In this aria, he denounces them all, and asks them for what price they sold her, his own priceless treasure. He tries to get past a closed door, but they manipulate him away from it. He begins to cry and puts emotional pressure on one courtier, Marullo. He asks, as an old man whose only interest in life is his daughter, for pity and pardon from them all.*

A good audition aria that lies very high, and needs power, line and declamation. The singer must be very aware of the cello obbligato in the last section, and the cor anglais parts in the accompaniment. For the optional high G, see Ricci, *Book of Cadenzas*.

**209. Il balen del suo sorriso** (Conte di Luna)
(Recit: Tutto è deserto)
Il trovatore (1853), Act I sc 2 no 12
Verdi [4'45"] 📖 EP4249

*Biscay, 15th century: Leonora, separated from her love, Manrico, has decided to enter a convent. The Count di Luna, also in love with her and an enemy of Manrico, enters the cloister grounds with the intention of kidnapping her. He sees that all is quiet, and expresses the love that burns inside him.*

A recitative and very taxing cavatina requiring a wonderful top to the voice. For the pianist, this is one of the hardest arias to accompany well. (See Ricci, *Book of Cadenzas*.)

**210. Eri tu** (Anckarstroem/Renato)
(Recit: Alzati!)
Un ballo in maschera (1859), Act III fig 7
Verdi [5'] 📖 EP4249

*Sweden, 1792: Count Anckarstroem (Renato) has assisted King Gustavo (Riccardo) in an assignation with his lover, only to discover that this person is his wife, Amelia. Back at home, the Count decides that she must die for her adultery, but she pleads to see her son for one last time. In the recitative, he allows this wish but sends her out to hide her shame. On being left alone, he realizes that Gustavo rather than Amelia is to blame, and that he must have vengeance. Gustavo has used his friendship with the Count for his own purpose. Although Anckarstroem has many happy memories of their friendship, he accepts that it is finished.*

A wide-ranging, big, dramatic aria, good for audition purposes, which demonstrates rich cantabile line and declamatory power. The melodic turns must be clearly sung both for the warmth of interpretation and so that the pianist can follow.

**211. Urna fatale** (Don Carlo)
(Recit: Morir! Tremenda cosa!)
La forza del destino (1862), Act III sc 2 no 20
Verdi [4'40"] 📖 EP4249

*Italy, 18th century: Don Carlo, Leonora's brother, is pursuing Leonora's lover, Alvaro, whom he thinks murdered his father. Don Carlo has enlisted in the Spanish army fighting in Italy, but, unknown to him, his captain is Alvaro himself. Alvaro is wounded and entrusts a casket to Don Carlo, ordering him never to open it. Don Carlo notices that Alvaro flinched at the family name of Calatrava and sings in this monologue of his temptation to open the casket.*

This heavy aria with a wide range should only be tackled by a baritone with great stamina and technique. The aria was originally in E major so, if it is printed in F major, transpose it down a semitone from the last ten bars of the recitative. It is not recommended that you sing the following cabaletta.

**212. Per me giunto è il dì supremo** (Rodrigo)
(Second part: O Carlo, ascolta)
(Recit: Son io, mio Carlo)
Don Carlo (Don Carlos) (1867), Act IV sc 2 (5-act version)
Verdi [3'30" + 3'20"]

1st part:      2nd part:

*Spain, mid-16th century: Rodrigo has looked after some revolutionary*
*papers from Flanders for Carlo at the end of Act III scene 1, and knows*
*that he will be arrested soon. He comes to say goodbye to Carlo (who is now*
*in prison) and tells him he will be safe. He sings that dying for a true*
*friend is the best sacrifice. After the first part, Carlo says he wants to confess*
*all in order to save Rodrigo's life, but Rodrigo says he must think only of*
*Flanders now. Suddenly Rodrigo is shot, and in the second half he whispers*
*that Don Carlo's mother, Elizabetta, will meet him at St Juste. Don Carlo*
*must save Flanders and, if Rodrigo's dying saves Spain, he will be happy.*

An aria showing off a splendid Verdian line. You can also cut to the
second part beginning at 'O Carlo, ascolta' but the result can seem
rather long, given that both sections have a broad line. This second part
demonstrates declamatory skill and singing of high lines. In the recitative, cut after 'Son io, mio Carlo' to 'Usir tu dei' with the two orchestral chords that precede it. The original language is French.

**213. Votre toast, je peux vous le rendre** (Escamillo)
Carmen (1875), Act II no 14 (or 13)
Bizet [4']   📖 EP7555

*Seville, 1820: Escamillo, a famous bull fighter, makes a grand entrance*
*into the local tavern. He describes the excitement of the fight and how the*
*reward is his señorita's love.*

This two-verse aria has a deceptively low range, needing strong tone at
the bottom. It is an awkward piece, which requires rich and powerful
singing. Watch the tricky intonation, as there should be much descrip-
tive story-telling, especially in the second verse. Cut from the end of the

first verse to the introduction to the second verse. At the end of the second verse, cut directly to the last eight bars of the number.

**214. Scintille diamant** (Dapertutto)
(Recit: Allez! Pour te livrer combat)
Les contes d'Hoffmann (1881), Act II no 15
Offenbach [2']

*Venice, 19th century: Dapertutto is intent on capturing another soul, using the charm of the courtesan, Giulietta, to get Hoffmann's reflection on to his mirror. He sings of the mirror which, like a decoy, attracts the 'lark' and captures it.*

This is a very concise aria, which shows off the top of the voice. It needs a good sinuous line. Often this aria is transposed down in performance but an audition panel would expect to hear it sung in E major.

**215. Vision fugitive** (Hérode)
(Recit: Ce breuvage pourrait)
Hérodiade (1881), Act II sc 5 fig 77
Massenet [2'50"] 📖 EP7555

*Jerusalem, first century AD: Herod has spotted Salome, but does not know that she is the daughter of his wife Herodiade. Herod cannot get her out of his mind and sings that he wishes to see her beauty again. He describes it as a fleeting vision, which he must follow.*

A high, passionately rich aria full of sweeping phrases, and a good audition piece. The notes marked with stress lines need full vowels to give them their full value. Massenet slightly overmarks the dynamics to encourage the singers of his day to sing with more colours, so take care that they sound organic. The pianist should help by allowing the tempo to be very flexible.

**216. Vanne; la tua meta già vedo – Credo** (Iago)

Otello (1887), Act II sc 2 letter C

Verdi [4'45"]

*Cyprus, end of 15th century: Iago, Othello's ensign, has manipulated the situation so that Cassio loses his position as lieutenant, and now has suggested to him to ask Desdemona, Othello's wife, to use her influence to get himself reinstated. As Cassio leaves, Iago, like Claggart in* Billy Budd, *sings his creed that he was born from evil, and is committed by his hateful god to destroying the idea of justice and heaven.*

A very strong, dramatic aria, full of dark, evil colours, demanding exciting declamation of the Italian text.

**217. Si può?** (Tonio)

I pagliacci (1892), Prologue

Leoncavallo [4'15"]

*Calabria, 1865–70: Tonio prepares the audience for the opera. The author has taken the story from life, and it is true in all its emotions.*

This good audition aria requires a fluent top to the voice and clear low notes. It also demands declamatory use of words, colours and line. The top A♭ and G are optional, but are usually expected to be sung:

al pa - ri di voi spi-ria-mo l'ae – re

and the penultimate syllable of 'Incominciate!' becomes a high G.

**218. È sogno? o realtà** (Ford)

Falstaff (1893), Act II sc 1 fig 19

Verdi [4'30"]

*Windsor, c.1400: Ford has come in disguise to the Garter Inn to find out from Falstaff when he has arranged his assignation with Mrs Ford. Ford*

*pretends to be in love with Mrs Ford, and wants Falstaff to prepare the way. With this flattery, Falstaff is tricked into telling the time of the arranged meeting. As Falstaff goes off to dress, Ford breaks into this angry monologue. He sees himself cuckolded and curses marriage and women, swearing vengeance for this outrage.*

A wonderful declamatory aria demanding lots of character and the stamina to cope with the big phrase at the end. There must be a real feeling of enjoyment in the enunciation of the Italian text. The piano accompaniment is a real tour de force.

**219. Nemico della Patria?!** (Gérard)
Andrea Chénier (1896), Act III fig 12
Giordano [4'15"]

*Paris, French Revolution: Gérard, a comrade of Chénier, who shares the same revolutionary views, has discovered that they are both in love with Maddalena. They have fought a duel without recognizing each other, but when Gérard was wounded he realized it was Chénier, and allowed him to escape. Incredible, a spy, asks him to sign an indictment against Chénier, who has now been arrested. In this monologue, Gérard is torn between his faithfulness to Chénier and his jealousy of Chénier's relationship with Maddalena.*

A declamatory aria full of contrasts, similar to the Prologue to *I pagliacci*. It is best to end at the words 'tutte le genti amar!'. There should be good contrast between the strong use of words in the first half and the melodic sweep of the section 'La coscienza nei cuor'.

**220. Nulla! Silenzio!** (Michele)
Il tabarro (1918), fig 86
Puccini [3']

*Paris, early-20th century: Michele, owner of a barge, suspects that his wife Giorgetta has a lover. In the evening he sits on the barge, knowing his wife is waiting for someone, but not knowing who it might be. He considers all the possibilities, and calls upon his wife's lover to face Michele's hatred and to die.*

A big, declamatory dramatic aria for which the singer needs good pacing, especially in terms of dynamics and energy.

# Heroic baritone

**221. Pietà, rispetto, amore** (Macbeth)
(Recit: Perfidi! All'Anglo contro me v'unite!)
Macbeth (1847/1865), Act IV sc 3 no 20
Verdi [4'15"]

*Scotland, 1040: Macbeth is furious that Malcolm is leading an army, including English troops, against him. He relies on the prophecy of the witches, that he cannot die from someone 'born of woman', and yet Macbeth is tired of life. He had hoped that love and honour would have stayed with him into old age, but when he dies, it is curses, not tears, that will fall on his head.*

A high-lying aria demanding strong singing and good firm line of voice. The recitative must be very dramatic.

**222. Mein Vater!** (Amfortas)
Parsifal (1882), Act III sc 2 fig 277
Wagner [4'30"]

*Holy Grail Castle, Spain, Middle Ages: Titurel, former ruler of the Grail, who had handed the office over to his son Amfortas, has just died. Amfortas was wounded by Klingsor and has since suffered from the wound, and desires to die as well. He asks Titurel, if he is near the Saviour, to entreat Him to bless the knights of the Grail and to let him die.*

A slow, intense aria requiring incredible control and understanding. A full use of the vowels of the German text will ensure that Amfortas's 'suffering' is expressed without any 'weeping' in the voice. It is best to end at the words 'gib meinem Sohne Ruh'!'.

## 223. Ni sna, ni otdikha izmuchennoi dushe
   (Prince Igor)
Prince Igor (1890), Act II no 13
Borodin [5'15"]  📖 EP7583

*Poutivil, 1185: Prince Igor is a prisoner of a Tartar tribe, which he had
set out to defeat. He sings of his homesickness and longs to go back to his
people in order to keep them safe. He remembers his wife, Yaroslavna, with
tenderness.*

A long, heavy aria requiring rich singing and much power. The accompaniment must not become too 'square'; the quavers should always
have a forward momentum.

# Russian Operatic Arias

Following the success of the *French Operatic Arias* series, Peters Edition is delighted to announce its next major opera aria project – *Russian Operatic Arias*, featuring a fascinating range of arias from this wonderful and often challenging pool of repertoire. Arias will be printed in their original language with clear transliteration, and each volume will include guidance on pronunciation.

These arias have been selected and edited by David Fanning, the well-known broadcaster, author, critic and lecturer. A specialist in Russian music, David Fanning is the area editor for Russian and Scandinavian music for the revised New Grove Dictionary of Music and Musicians.

| Russian Operatic Arias for Soprano | EP 7580 | in preparation |
| Russian Operatic Arias for Mezzo-Soprano | EP 7581 | in preparation |
| Russian Operatic Arias for Tenor | EP 7582 | in preparation |
| Russian Operatic Arias for Baritone | EP 7583 | in preparation |
| Russian Operatic Arias for Bass | EP 7584 | in preparation |

# Bass arias

## Buffo bass

**224. Solche hergelaufne Laffen** (Osmin)
Die Entführung aus dem Serail (1782), Act I no 3
Mozart [4'15" omitting Allegro assai] 📖 EP737

*Turkey, 16th century: Osmin, the harem's overseer, does not like Pedrillo who works for him because he is a rival for Blonde's love. When Pedrillo confronts him, he vents his rage on him, telling him that he knows what he is up to, and that no-one ever tricks Osmin.*

A declamatory aria with much text, always to be phrased in one in a bar, and needing rhythmic singing. There are only two melismas, both on the word 'Laffen', and they should have clearly sung trills and accurate chromatic scales, leaving the accents to the orchestra. It is best to end before the Allegro assai.

**225. La vendetta** (Bartolo)
(Recit: Bene, io tutto farò)
Le nozze di Figaro (1786), Act I no 4
Mozart [3'] 📖 EP737, EP8903, EP4235

*Seville, 18th century: Bartolo promises to help Marcellina (who has a contract to marry Figaro if he does not repay a loan), partly to get rid of her,*

*because he still feels guilty over their past relationship. He realizes that the best way to catch out Figaro is not through vengeance, but through his lawyer's guile.*

This aria has quite a big range and a mixture of strong declamatory singing and fast 'patter'. Begin from the end of the recitative, with the pianist overlapping the final chord with the beginning of the aria. Be careful not to accent the text too much – Mozart brings out the important words by lengthening the note-values.

**226. Madamina! – Catalogue Aria** (Leporello)
(Recit: Eh consolatevi)
Don Giovanni (1787), Act I no 4
Mozart [5'50"]  📖 EP737, EP8903, EP4235

*Seville, 17th century: Leporello and Donna Elvira have been abandoned by Don Giovanni. Leporello is left to console Donna Elvira who is in a distraught state, having been searching for Don Giovanni for weeks. Leporello distracts her thoughts by showing her his catalogue of Don Giovanni's amorous conquests, all noted down in great detail.*

A useful audition aria demonstrating declamation and different colours over the orchestra's excited accompaniment, which illustrates Donna Elvira's shock at hearing about Don Giovanni's catalogue (always keep in mind the immorality of the whole aria). In the minuet section the line is important to allow Leporello to demonstrate his desire to sing as well as an aristocrat. It is best to begin at the end of the secco recitative.

**227. When my cue comes – Bottom's Dream** (Bottom)
A Midsummer Night's Dream (1960), Act III fig 25
Britten [4'10"]

*A wood near Athens, legendary: Bottom has just woken up, now without his ass's head and, as in a dream, remembers vaguely where he should have been. He recalls his cue in the rustics' play, but also his strange dream. He will get Peter Quince to write a ballad about this dream, to sing to the Duke.*

This declamatory aria is difficult musically and has much colour varia-tion. Remember that, as Bottom is a weaver, his thoughts must weave languidly through the music as he recalls, with difficulty, his dream. This is very hard for the pianist, especially the second half, and a good way to end the aria needs to be found. Figure 32 should have a feeling of quintuplets within the dotted rhythms.

# Bass-baritone

**228. Se vuol ballare** (Figaro)
(Recit: Bravo, Signor padrone!)
Le nozze di Figaro (1786), Act I no 3
Mozart [3'5"] 📖 EP737, EP8903

*Near Seville, 18th century: Figaro has discovered from his wife-to-be, Susanna, that the reason the Count has arranged his room next to their bridal suite is that he too desires Susanna. Figaro now understands why she has been chosen as 'confidential attaché' to the Count. Figaro sings that, not only will he play the game, he will also call the tune.*

A lively aria needing lots of energy, cynicism, good diction and 'springy' tone. Treat the Allegretto as an aristocratic dance and the Presto as a contrasting peasant dance – the battle of the classes thus begins!

**229. Non più andrai** (Figaro)
Le nozze di Figaro (1786), Act I no 9
Mozart [3'20" with shortened playout]
📖 EP737, EP8903, EP4235

*Near Seville, 18th century: The Count has just punished Cherubino for his flirtations by sending him to join the army. Figaro starts to tease Cherubino about his new life, and portrays a cynical view of war.*

A martial aria, which requires resonant diction, cynical humour and lots of bite. It is a good piece for character. Begin in the recitative at: 'Ehi, capitano'. The text needs to be phrased in one in a bar and be

well shaped. The section beginning 'schioppo in spalla' has a feeling of
an accompanied recitative.

**230. Aprite un po' quegl'occhi** (Figaro)
(Recit: Tutto è disposto)
Le nozze di Figaro (1786), Act IV no 26
Mozart [3'45"]  EP737, EP4235

*Near Seville, 18th century: Figaro noticed the Count reading a secret letter
sealed with a pin. Now he discovers that Barbarina has been ordered to
take back this pin to Susanna, Figaro's wife, so Figaro believes his wife is
responsible for the letter. In this aria, like Guglielmo in* Così fan tutte *(see
No. 192), Figaro sings about woman's unfaithfulness.*

This aria has much text, thus requiring good diction and good pacing
to prevent it sounding repetitive. Imagine that it is sung directly to the
audience, with the repetitions addressed to different parts of the room.

**231. La calunnia** (Basilio)
Il barbiere di Siviglia (1816), Act I no 6
Rossini [3'45" with cut]  EP737, EP4235

*Seville, 17th century: Basilio, music master to Rosina, advises her guardian,
Dr Bartolo, that Count Almaviva is in town and probably has been wooing Rosina. He says that the way to get rid of him is by spreading a slan-
derous story about him. In the aria, he explains that slander is, at the
beginning, like a gentle wind, and then grows into a storm as it spreads
through the town.*

This buffo aria lies quite high, with sections in which it is hard to sort
out the breathing. You might best be advised to leave out the repeat of
the section 'E il meschino calunniato' and cut to the final eight bars of
singing. This aria is usually sung in C major.

**232.** **Le veau d'or est toujours debout! –**
    **Song of the Golden Calf** (Méphistophélès)

Faust (1859), Act II no 4
Gounod [2'10"]   EP7556

*Germany, 16th century: Mephistopheles interrupts Wagner's song in the tavern by singing this cynical song about Man's worship of the golden calf.*

A two-verse aria which lies quite high and yet needs a bass quality. It can be very tiring to sing, and the pacing demands a good technique. The narrative aspect must be well in evidence.

**233.** **O beauty, O handsomeness, goodness** (Claggart)

Billy Budd (1951), Act I sc 3 fig 105
Britten [5'15"]

*HMS Indomitable, 1797: John Claggart, Master of Arms, has taken on a personal battle with Billy Budd, a new recruit. He has recognized in Billy a beauty that he hates and, like Iago, states his creed that he must destroy it.*

An aria which demands power, evil and use of words and line to the voice. In the first and last sections, the text is set very slowly, so give all the syllables their full due. Notice how many phrases are marked by Britten with legato phrase-marks. The middle quick section must be accurately sung but should still have an element of danger. It is probably good to begin at 'Handsome indeed …', a few bars before fig 105, and end at fig 111.

# Basso profondo

**234.** **O Isis and Osiris** (Sarastro)

Die Zauberflöte (1791), Act II no 10
Mozart [2'30"]   EP4235, EP737

*Egypt, legendary: Sarastro prays to the Egyptian gods to keep Tamino and his companion safe as they undergo their temple trials.*

A famous audition aria requiring sustained singing and rich tone.

**235. In diesen heil'gen Hallen** (Sarastro)
Die Zauberflöte (1791), Act II no 15
Mozart [3'30"] 📖 EP4235, EP8903, EP737

*Egypt, legendary: Pamina pleads for her mother, who has been conspiring to achieve Sarastro's death, but Sarastro preaches that her punishment will be carried out through the power of love, this being the creed of the temple.*

A good, two-verse aria requiring good intonation and steady tone. It is possible to go down to low E at the end, but it is in slightly poor taste.

**236. Vi ravviso, o luoghi ameni** (Conte Rodolfo)
(Cabaletta: Tu non sai)
La sonnambula (1831), Act 1 no 6
Bellini [2'15" + 2'20" one verse and with cut]

*Switzerland, early-19th century: Rodolfo unknown to the villagers, is the Lord of the Castle and, on his arrival, remembers his youth in the village. He meets Amina, just betrothed to Elvino, and tells her how she reminds him of a past love in his youth.*

A *basso cantante* aria, which requires good tone and well-sung dotted rhythms and triplets. Use the transition from cavatina to cabaletta and then sing only one verse. Also cut the first eight bars of the Più mosso. (See Ricci, *Book of Cadenzas*.)

**237. Infelice! … e tuo credevi** (Silva)
(Recit: Che mai vegg'io!)
Ernani (1844), Act I finale
Verdi [2'30"] 📖 EP4245

*Spain, early-16th century: Elvira, Silva's intended wife, has discovered the King of Castile in her room, declaring his love for her. Ernani, also her lover and a rebel Chief, has just arrived and has accosted the king. Now Silva arrives and discovers Elvira with two lovers! In the recitative, he describes the scene as it appears to him and calls in his knights to be witnesses. In the cavatina, he sings to himself of the delusions that he had – that this young girl was going to be wife to him, an unhappy old man.*

A cantabile aria with a short recitative, which shows off flexibility of voice and range, often within the same phrase.

**238. O tu, Palermo** (Procida)
   I vespri Siciliani (1855), Act II no 7
   Verdi [4'] 📖 EP4245

*Palermo, 1282: Giovanni da Procida, a Sicilian doctor, who is secretly returning home to stir up resistance against French occupation, sings of his love for his country.*

A slow, bel canto aria requiring a rich quality of voice. The small appoggiaturas should be well sung, and good use should be made of the tenuto accents. The cadenza can be shortened. The original language is French.

**239. Il lacerato spirito** (Fiesco)
   (Recit: A te l'estremo addio)
   Simon Boccanegra (1857), Prologue letter P
   Verdi [3'20"]

*Genoa, 14th century: Fiesco, the Doge of Genoa, has just come from the death-bed of his daughter, who was in love with Boccanegra and bore him a daughter. Fiesco bids an emotional farewell to the sepulchral palace. He asks the Virgin Mary why she allowed his daughter to be seduced and then asks pardon for his words. His spirit is torn by sorrow and, when he hears the mourners lamenting, he can only turn for help to the Virgin.*

A very good audition aria which shows off a good range. It is slow but has a dramatic recitative.

**240. Come dal ciel precipita** (Banco)
   (Recit: Studia il passo, o mio figlio!)
   Macbeth (1847/1865), Act II sc 2 no 10
   Verdi [4'] 📖 EP4245

*Scotland, 1040: The witches prophesied that Banco's descendants would be future kings of Scotland. Macbeth has murdered the king to gain the throne*

*and, because of this prophecy, resolves to have Banco and his son murdered as well. Banco is walking with his son in a park at night, and he has the same feeling as he did on the night that King Duncan died. After the aria, he is killed by the assassins, but his son escapes.*

A very good, concise audition aria demonstrating legato singing, good range and richness of voice. The pianist should note the heaviness of the orchestration in this aria.

**241. Ella giammai m'amò!** (Filippo)
Don Carlo (Don Carlos) (1867),
 Act IV sc 1 (5-act version)
Verdi [6' with short intro.]  EP4245

*Spain, mid-16th century: At night, King Philip II, in this great monologue, comes to terms with the fact that his wife never loved him. He saw it when he first brought her back from France. Now he sees the dawn light filtering through the window, and feels, in the same way, his own life ebbing away. When he dies, he will lie alone in the vault. If his worldly power could let him read a human heart, it could tell him whether Don Carlo sleeps or if the traitor is awake.*

A marvellous, wide-ranging aria demonstrating declamatory power, line and a feeling for drama. A feeling of the weight of authority must always be apparent in the interpretation. The original language is French.

**242. Lyubvi vse vozrasti pakorni** (Gremin)
Eugene Onegin (1879), Act III sc 1 no 20A
Tchaikovsky [5'30"]  EP7584

*St Petersburg, late-18th century: Prince Gremin has been married to Tatyana for two years when Onegin, Tatyana's first love, arrives at Gremin's house. At the ball, Onegin asks Gremin, an old friend and distant relation, who the lady is that he thinks he recognizes. Gremin says that she is his wife and then in the aria proceeds to tell him of her beauty and charm, and how she makes him feel young again.*

A wonderful audition aria, showing off line and range. The contrast between Gremin's bitter view of the world and his admiration of his wife must be clearly made in the middle section. If the aria is sung in Russian, make sure that the syllable on the F in bar 22 is not pronounced with an 'o' vowel, since the phrase will then translate as 'Onegin, I do not get out of bed'!

**243. Vecchia zimarra** (Colline)
    La bohème (1896), Act IV fig 19
    Puccini [1'50"]

*Paris, 1830: Mimì has arrived at the men's home mortally ill, and Musetta and Marcello have gone out to get a doctor and to bring back Mimì's muff. Colline sings this emotional aria to his coat, deciding he must sell it. He recalls its life, how it never bent its back to the rich and powerful, and he remembers all the philosophical and poetical books that lived in its pockets. He finally bids his coat a friendly goodbye.*

A short, perfect miniature which demonstrates line, phrasing and warm singing.

# The Peters Edition Lieder Guide

The Peters Edition Lieder Guide is an exhaustive resource of information designed to assist and encourage innovative programme planning by singers, teachers, accompanists and artistic directors, and contains:

## Lieder and Song section
- songs listed by Peters Edition volume contents
- songs listed by title, with an easy cross-reference to the Peters Edition volume contents section
- indication of keys and ranges available for each song
- date of composition, name of poet, indication of original language and list of translations available for each song from Peters Edition

## Opera Aria section
- arias listed by Peters Edition volume contents
- arias listed by title and opera, with easy cross-reference to Peters Edition volume contents section
- details of translations available from Peters Edition

Catalogue Number  EP 7603

# Part III
# Index of Audition Arias

Here follows an extensive list of audition arias, listed by composer, within the five voice types (Soprano, Mezzo-soprano, Tenor, Baritone and Bass). You will be able to see at a glance to which *Fach* a specific aria belongs. This will give you some idea of the wide choice of audition arias open to you. Those that I highly recommend for audition purposes have already been treated in depth in Part II and can be traced through their aria number. Others, available in Peters Edition, are given with their catalogue (EP) number.

# Soprano arias

**S** = Soubrette
**LC** = Lyric coloratura
**L** = Lyric
**DC** = Dramatic coloratura

**JD** = Spinto (Jugendlich-Dramatischer)
**D** = Dramatic
**HD** = Heavy dramatic

**\*** = Long aria (which may need to be cut)
**SI** = Short introduction and/or playout
Cabaletta or recitative title in brackets

| Voice | Composer | Aria title | Character | Opera (Act/No.) | Aria No. |
|-------|----------|-----------|-----------|-----------------|----------|
| LC | Auber | Quel bonheur, je respire | Zerline | *Fra Diavolo* (III/7) 3'30" | 15 |
| L | Barber | Do not utter a word | Vanessa | *Vanessa* (I/fig 22–27) 2'50" | 48 |
| S | Beethoven | O wär'ich schon mit dir vereint | Marzelline | *Fidelio* (I/2) 4' | 5 |
| D | Beethoven | Abscheulicher! wo eilst du hin? | Fidelio | *Fidelio* (I/9) 6'30" | 88 |
| L | Bellini | Oh! quante volte | Giulietta | *I Capuleti e i Montecchi* (I/4) 5'45" | 37 |
| DC* | Bellini | Casta diva (Ah, bello a me ritorno) | Norma | *Norma* (I/4) 5'15" (SI) +2'30" (1v) | 58 |
| DC* | Bellini | Qui la voce sua soave (Vien, diletto) | Elvira | *I puritani* (II/fig 24) 2'35" + 2'30" (1v SI) | 61 |

| | | | | | |
|---|---|---|---|---|---|
| DC* | Bellini | Ah! non credea mirarti (Ah! Non giunge) | Amina | La sonnambula (III/14) 3'30" + 1'45" (1v) | 59 |
| LC* | Bernstein | Glitter and be gay | Cunegonde | Candide (I/7) 3'45" (cut) | 30 |
| L | Bizet | Je dis que rien ne m'épouvante | Micaëla | Carmen (III/22) 4'30" | 39 |
| L | Bizet | Comme autrefois dans la nuit sombre | Leïla | Les pêcheurs de perles (II/7) 5' | 38 |
| DC | Boito | L'altra notte in fonde al mare | Margherita | Mefistofele (III) 3'15" | 68 |
| L | Britten | Embroidery Aria | Ellen | Peter Grimes (III/fig 23) 3'10" | 47 |
| LC | Britten | Come, now a roundel | Tytania | A Midsummer Night's Dream (I/fig 94) 2'5" | 31 |
| JD | Britten | How beautiful it is (Tower Scene) | Governess | The Turn of the Screw (I/sc 4/7 after fig 22) 4'30" | – |
| L | Catalani | Ebben? ... Ne andrò lontana | La Wally | La Wally (I/letter Q) 3'30" | 40 |
| JD | Cilea | Io son l'umile ancella | Adriana | Adriana Lecouvreur (I/fig 13) 2'30" | 85 |
| S | Charpentier | Depuis le jour | Louise | Louise (III/1) 4' | 8 |
| LC | Delibes | Où va la jeune Hindoue? – Bell song | Lakmé | Lakmé (II/10) 6'45" | 26 |
| DC | Donizetti | Il faut partir | Marie | La fille du régiment (I/13) 2'45" (1v) | 62 |
| LC | Donizetti | O luce di quest'anima | Linda | Linda di Chamounix (I/4) 4'30" | 16 |
| DC | Donizetti | Regnava nel silenzio | Lucia | Lucia di Lammermoor (I/2) 3'10" + 4'15" (SI) | 60 |
| LC | Donizetti | Quel guardo il cavaliere | Norina | Don Pasquale (I/sc 2/no 3) 5'45" | 17 |
| L | Dvořák | Měsíčku na nebi – Song to the moon | Rusalka | Rusalka (I/fig 39) 4'10" | 43 |
| JD | Giordano | La mamma morta | Maddalena | Andrea Chénier (III/fig 23) 4' | 84 |
| JD | Gluck | Divinités du Styx | Alceste | Alceste (I/7) 3'50" | 71 |
| JD | Gluck | Ô malheureuse Iphigénie | Iphigénie | Iphigénie en Tauride (II/sc 6) 3'15" | EP 734 |
| DC | Gounod | Ah, je ris de me voir – Air des bijoux | Marguerite | Faust (III/9) 4'45" | 67 |

| Voice | Composer | Aria title | Character | Opera (Act/No.) | Aria No. |
|---|---|---|---|---|---|
| LC | Gounod | O légère hirondelle | Mireille | *Mireille* (I/1A) 3'30" | EP 7552 |
| LC | Gounod | Je veux vivre | Juliette | *Roméo et Juliette* (I/3) 3'15" | 23 |
| LC | Handel | Tornami a vagheggiar | Morgana | *Alcina* (I/end) 5' | 11 |
| LC | Handel | Ah! spietato! (Il crudel m'abbandona) | Melissa | *Amadigi* (I/sc 4) 5'30" | EP 3493 |
| LC | Handel | Svegliatevi nel core | Sesto | *Giulio Cesare* (I/5) 4'5" | – |
| LC* | Handel | Se pietà di me non senti (Che sento!) | Cleopatra | *Giulio Cesare* (II/27) 8'45" | EP4231a |
| LC | Handel | Piangerò la sorte mia | Cleopatra | *Giulio Cesare* (III/sc 3/no 32) 5'15" | 10 |
| LC | Leoncavallo | Stridono lassù (Ballatella) | Nedda | *I pagliacci* (I/fig 36) 4'40" | 29 |
| L | Mascagni | Son pochi fiori | Suzel | *L'amico Fritz* (I/fig 7) 2'30" | – |
| JD | Mascagni | Voi lo sapete, o mamma | Santuzza | *Cavalleria rusticana* (no 5) 3'40" | 80 |
| JD | Massenet | Pleurez! Pleurez, mes yeux! | Chimène | *Le Cid* (III/fig 228) 4'45" | 78 |
| JD | Massenet | Il est doux, il est bon (Celui dont la parole) | Salomé | *Hérodiade* (I) 4'30" | – |
| LC | Massenet | Adieu, notre petite table | Manon | *Manon* (II/fig 123) 3'15" | 27 |
| LC | Massenet | Je marche sur tous les chemins (Gavotte) | Manon | *Manon* (III/fig 189) 5'15" | 28 |
| S | Massenet | Frère! voyez! | Sophie | *Werther* (II/fig 105) 2' | – |
| L | Menotti | Up in the sky someone is playing a trombone (Bravo) | Monica | *The Medium* (II/4 before fig 2) 4'40". | – |
| D* | Menotti | To this we've come (Papers! Papers!) | Magda | *The Consul* (I/sc 2/fig 96 & 3 before 103) 2'20" + 4' | – |
| LC | Meyerbeer | Air du sommeil (Sur mes genoux) | Sélika | *L'Africaine* (II/4) 5'30" | – |

| | Composer | Aria | Character | Opera | EP 2074 |
|---|---|---|---|---|---|
| LC* | Meyerbeer | Ombre légère qui suis mes pas | Dinorah | Dinorah (II/15) 6'45" | |
| DC | Meyerbeer | Robert, toi que j'aime | Isabelle | Robert le diable (IV/18) 4'45" | – |
| L* | Mozart | Non più di fiori vaghe catene | Vitellia | La clemenza di Tito (II/sc 2/no 23) 6'45" | 35 |
| S | Mozart | In uomini, in soldati | Despina | Così fan tutte (I/12) 2'25" | 3 |
| DC | Mozart | Come scoglio | Fiordiligi | Così fan tutte (I/14) 5'10" | 53 |
| S | Mozart | Una donna a quindici anni | Despina | Così fan tutte (II/19) 3'15" | 4 |
| DC | Mozart | Ach ich liebte, war so glücklich | Konstanze | Die Entführung aus dem Serail (I/6) 5' | 50 |
| LC | Mozart | Durch Zärtlichkeit and Schmeicheln | Blonde | Die Entführung aus dem Serail (II/8) 3' (short vers.) | 14 |
| DC | Mozart | Traurigkeit | Konstanze | Die Entführung aus dem Serail (II/10) 6'25" | – |
| DC* | Mozart | Martern aller Arten | Konstanze | Die Entführung aus dem Serail (II/11) 6'45" | EP4231a /EP2074 |
| LC | Mozart | Welche Wonne, welche Lust | Blonde | Die Entführung aus dem Serail (II/12) 2'45" (short vers.) | EP4231a /EP734 |
| DC | Mozart | Or sai chi l'onore (Allora rinforzo) | Donna Anna | Don Giovanni (I/10) 3'45" | 51 |
| S | Mozart | Batti, batti, o bel Masetto (Ma se colpo) | Zerlina | Don Giovanni (I/13) 4'20" | 2 |
| S | Mozart | Vedrai, carino | Zerlina | Don Giovanni (II/19) 2'45" (SI) | EP4245/EP4231a /EP734 |
| L | Mozart | Mi tradì quell'alma ingrata | Donna Elvira | Don Giovanni (II/23) 5'30" | 34 |
| DC | Mozart | Non mi dir, bell'idol mio | Donna Anna | Don Giovanni (II/25) 6'10" | 52 |
| LC | Mozart | Padre! germani! addio! | Ilia | Idomeneo (I/1) 4'10" | 12 |

| Voice | Composer | Aria title | Character | Opera (Act/No.) | Aria No. |
|---|---|---|---|---|---|
| LC | Mozart | Zeffiretti lusinghieri (Solitudine amiche) | Ilia | Idomeneo (III/16 or 19) 6' | 13 |
| DC | Mozart | D'Oreste, d'Ajace! (Oh smania!) | Electra | Idomeneo (III/24 or 29) 5'10" | 49 |
| L | Mozart | Porgi amor | Contessa | Le nozze di Figaro (II/10) 2'10" (SI) | 32 |
| L | Mozart | Dove sono | Contessa | Le nozze di Figaro (III/19) 5'30" | 33 |
| S | Mozart | Deh vieni, non tardar | Susanna | Le nozze di Figaro (IV/27) 3'30" | 1 |
| LC | Mozart | L'amerò, sarò costante | Aminta | Il rè pastore (II/10) 4'50" | – |
| LC | Mozart | Ruhe sanft | Zaïde | Zaïde (I/3) 5'30" (in G) | – |
| DC | Mozart | O zitt're nicht, mein lieber Sohn! | Königen der Nacht | Die Zauberflöte (I/4) 4'35" | 54 |
| DC | Mozart | Der Hölle Rache | Königen der Nacht | Die Zauberflöte (II/14) 3'10" | 55 |
| L | Mozart | Ach, ich fühl's | Pamina | Die Zauberflöte (II/17) 3'30" | 36 |
| DC* | Nicolai | Verführer! | Frau Fluth | Die lustigen Weiber von Windsor (I/sc 2/no 3) 5'50" (cut) | 64 |
| LC* | Nicolai | Wohl denn! gefasst ist der Entschluss | Anna Reich | Die lustigen Weiber von Windsor (III/11) 5'30" (SI) | 18 |
| LC | Offenbach | Les oiseaux dans la charmille – Doll song | Olympia | Les contes d'Hoffmann (I/9A or 12) 5'20" | EP7552 |
| L | Offenbach | Elle a fui, la tourterelle | Antonia | Les contes d'Hoffmann (III/18 or 25) 3' | EP7552 |
| JD | Ponchielli | Suicidio! | La Gioconda | La Gioconda (IV) 3'20" | 77 |
| S | Poulenc | Non, monsieur, mon mari | Thérèse | Les mamelles de Tirésias (I/fig 20) 5'15" | 9 |

| | | | | | |
|---|---|---|---|---|---|
| JD | Puccini | Senza mamma, o bimbo | Angelica | *Suor Angelica* (fig 60) 4' | 87 |
| L | Puccini | Sì. Mi chiamono Mimì | Mimì | *La bohème* (I/fig 35) 4' | 41 |
| S | Puccini | Quando me'n vo' | Musetta | *La bohème* (II/fig 21) 2'25" | 7 |
| L | Puccini | Donde lieta uscì al tuo grido d'amore | Mimì | *La bohème* (III/fig 26) 2'30" | 42 |
| JD | Puccini | Un bel dì, vedremo | Butterfly | *Madama Butterfly* (II/fig 12) 4' | 86 |
| JD | Puccini | Che tua madre dovrà prenderti in braccio | Butterfly | *Madama Butterfly* (II/fig 54) 3'20" | – |
| L | Puccini | Oh! mio babbino caro | Lauretta | *Gianni Schicchi* (fig 40) 2' | 44 |
| JD | Puccini | In quelle trine morbide | Manon | *Manon Lescaut* (II/fig 6) 2' | 82 |
| JD | Puccini | Sola ... perduta ... abbandonata | Manon | *Manon Lescaut* (IV/fig 10) 4'15" | 83 |
| L | Puccini | Chi'l bel sogno di Doretta | Magda | *La rondine* (I/fig 12) 2'30" | – |
| D | Puccini | Vissi d'arte | Tosca | *Tosca* (II/fig 51) 2'50" | 94 |
| L | Puccini | Signore ascolta! | Liù | *Turandot* (I/fig 42) 2'10" | 45 |
| HD | Puccini | In questa reggia | Turandot | *Turandot* (II/sc 2/fig 43) 6' | 96 |
| L | Puccini | Tu, che di gel sei cinta | Liù | *Turandot* (III/sc 1/fig 27) 2'10" | 46 |
| LC | Ravel | Air du feu (Arrière!) | Le Feu | *L'enfant et les sortilèges* (fig 39) 2' | – |
| DC | Rossini | Bel raggio lusinghier | Semiramide | *Semiramide* (I/7) 6' (SI) | 56 |
| DC | Rossini | Sombre forêt | Matilda | *Guillaume Tell* (II/sc 2/no 9) 3'30" | EP7552 |
| JD | Smetana | Ten lásky sen, jak krásný byl! | Mařenka | *The Bartered Bride* (III/sc 6) 4'50" | 76 |
| DC | J. Strauss | Klänge der Heimat – Csárdás | Rosalinde | *Die Fledermaus* (II/10) 4' | 69 |
| LC | J. Strauss | Audition Aria (Spiel'ich die Unschuld) | Adele | *Die Fledermaus* (III/14) 4'30" | 24 |
| D | R. Strauss | Es gibt ein Reich | Ariadne | *Ariadne auf Naxos* (fig 60) 5'15" | 95 |

| Voice | Composer | Aria title | Character | Opera (Act/No.) | Aria No. |
|---|---|---|---|---|---|
| LC* | R. Strauss | Grossmächtige Prinzessin | Zerbinetta | Ariadne auf Naxos (fig 100) 12'10" (Begin Allegretto mosso 8'10", begin Rondo 4') | — |
| HD* | R. Strauss | Monologue (Allein! Weh, ganz allein) | Elektra | Elektra (3 bef. fig 35 to fig 63) 9'40" | — |
| DC | Stravinsky | No word from Tom (My Father!) | Anne Truelove | The Rake's Progress (II/sc 3/fig 179) 3'45" + 4'15" | 70 |
| JD* | Tchaikovsky | Letter scene | Tatyana | Eugene Onegin (I/9) 13'30" | EP7580 |
| JD | Tchaikovsky | Uzh polnoch blizitsya | Lisa | Queen of Spades (III/20) 4' | 81 |
| S | Tippett | Oh my face – they say a woman's glory | Bella | The Midsummer Marriage (II/sc 3/fig 241) 3'45" | — |
| LC | Thomas | Je suis Titania | Philene | Mignon (II/sc 2/12C) 5' | 22 |
| D | Verdi | Ritorna vincitor! | Aida | Aida (I) 5'45" | 93 |
| D | Verdi | Qui Radames verrà | Aida | Aida (III) 5'35" | EP4246b |
| LC | Verdi | Volta la terrea | Oscar | Un ballo in maschera (I/sc 1/fig 21) 1'45" | 20 |
| D | Verdi | Ecco l'orrido campo | Amelia | Un ballo in maschera (II/fig 6) 6'10" (SI) | 89 |
| LC | Verdi | Saper vorreste | Oscar | Un ballo in maschera (III/sc 2/fig 53) 1'50" | 21 |
| JD* | Verdi | Tu che la vanità conoscesti del mondo | Elisabetta | Don Carlo (V) 8'30" | — |
| DC | Verdi | Ernani! Ernani, involami (Tutto sprezzo) | Elvira | Ernani (I/fig 16) 3'45' + 2' (1v) | 63 |
| S | Verdi | Sul fil d'un soffio etesio | Nannetta | Falstaff (III/sc 2/fig 35) 4'15" | 6 |
| D* | Verdi | Madre, pietosa vergine (Son giunta) | Leonora | La forza del destino (II/sc 2/no 12) 6'20" | 90 |
| D | Verdi | Pace, mio Dio | Leonora | La forza del destino (IV/sc 2/no 33) 5'20' | 91 |
| DC | Verdi | Qual prodigio! | Giselda | I Lombardi (IV/sc 1) 3'25" | — |

| | | | | | |
|---|---|---|---|---|---|
| D | Verdi | Vieni! t'affretta (Or tutti sorgete) | Lady Macbeth | *Macbeth* (I/sc 2/no 4) 4'10" (SI) + 2'40" (1v) | 92 |
| D | Verdi | La luce langue | Lady Macbeth | *Macbeth* (II/sc 1/no 8) 4'10" | EP4246a |
| D* | Verdi | Una macchia – Sleep-walking scene | Lady Macbeth | *Macbeth* (IV/sc 2/no 19) 6'45" | EP4246a |
| JD | Verdi | Piangea cantando – Willow song | Desdemona | *Otello* (IV/letter E–Q) 6' | 79 |
| LC | Verdi | Caro nome | Gilda | *Rigoletto* (I/sc 2) 4'45" | 19 |
| JD | Verdi | Come in quest'ora bruna | Amelia | *Simon Boccanegra* (I) 3'50" | – |
| DC* | Verdi | Ah, fors'è lui (Sempre libera) | Violetta | *La traviata* (I/6) 5'45" (1v) | 65 |
| DC | Verdi | Addio, del passato (Attendo) | Violetta | *La traviata* (III/16) 3' (1v) | EP4246b |
| JD | Verdi | Tacea la notte placida (Di tale amor) | Leonora | *Il trovatore* (I/4) 3'30" + 1'50" (1v) | 75 |
| JD | Verdi | D'amor sull'ali rosse vanne | Leonora | *Il trovatore* (IV/19) | EP4246b |
| DC | Verdi | Mercè, dilette amiche | Elena | *I vespri Siciliani* (V/fig 12) 2'40" (1v) | 66 |
| JD* | Wagner | Jo ho hoe – Senta's Ballad | Senta | *Der fliegende Holländer* (II/4A) 6' | – |
| JD | Wagner | Einsam in trüben Tagen – Elsa's Dream | Elsa | *Lohengrin* (I/fig 15) 5'40" | 74 |
| JD | Wagner | Dich, teure Halle | Elizabeth | *Tannhäuser* (II/sc 1) 3'20" | 73 |
| JD | Walton | At the haunted end of the day (How can I sleep?) | Cressida | *Troilus and Cressida* (II/fig 22) 4' | – |
| JD* | Weber | Leise, leise | Agathe | *Der Freischütz* (II/8) 8' | 72 |
| LC | Weber | Einst träumte meiner sel'gen Base | Ännchen | *Der Freischütz* (III/13) 5'40" | 106 |
| DC* | Weber | Ocean! thou mighty monster | Reiza | *Oberon* (II/13) 8'45" | 57 |

# Mezzo-soprano arias

L = Lyric
D = Dramatic
A = Contralto

\* = Long aria (which may need to be cut)
SI = Short introduction and/or playout

Cabaletta or recitative title in brackets

| Voice | Composer | Aria title | Character | Opera (Act/No.) | Aria No. |
|---|---|---|---|---|---|
| L | Barber | Must the winter come so soon? | Erika | Vanessa (I/fig 15–17) 2'15" | 113 |
| D* | Berlioz | Il m'en souvient | Béatrice | Béatrice et Bénédict (II/10) 4'10" (cut) | 117 |
| D* | Berlioz | D'amour l'ardente flamme | Marguerite | La damnation de Faust (IV/sc 15) 9'10" | EP7553 |
| D | Berlioz | Ah! Je vais mourir | Didon | Les troyens (V/sc 2/no 47) 5'35" | 118 |
| D | Bizet | L'amour est un oiseau rebelle – Habanera | Carmen | Carmen (I/5) 2'50" | 121 |
| D | Bizet | Près des remparts de Séville – Seguidilla | Carmen | Carmen (I/10 or 9) 2'10" | 122 |
| D | Britten | Flowers bring to ev'ry year (Give him this orchid) | Lucretia | The Rape of Lucretia (II/sc 2/fig 71) 3'20" | 129 |
| D | Cilea | Acerba voluttà | Principessa | Adriana Lecouvreur (II/fig 1) 4' | 127 |

| | | | | | |
|---|---|---|---|---|---|
| L | Donizetti | Ah! parea che per incanto (E sgombro il loco) | Smeton | *Anna Bolena* (I/7) 4'40" | – |
| D* | Donizetti | O mio Fernando! | Leonora | *La favorita* (III/fig 15) 5'50" (1v) | 116 |
| D | Gluck | Par un père cruel | Clytemnestre | *Iphigénie en Aulide* (II/sc 4/no 31) 2'40" | – |
| D | Gluck | Che farò senza Euridice | Orfeo | *Orfeo ed Euridice* (III/43) 4'30" | 114 |
| L | Gounod | Faites-lui mes aveux | Siebel | *Faust* (III/7) 3'10" | 108 |
| L | Gounod | Si le bonheur à sourire t'invite | Siebel | *Faust* (IV/12) 2' | – |
| L | Gounod | Que fais-tu, blanche tourterelle (Depuis hier) | Stéphano | *Roméo et Juliette* (III/12) 3'50" | EP7553 |
| L | Granados | La Maya y el Ruiseñor | Rosario | *Goyescas* (Sc 3) 4'50" | 112 |
| L | Handel | Where shall I fly | Dejanira | *Hercules* (III) 6'15" | – |
| L | Handel | Cara sposa | Rinaldo | *Rinaldo* (I/version in Em) 6'40" | – |
| D | Massenet | Werther ... Werther (Letter Scene) | Charlotte | *Werther* (III/fig 143) 6'20" | 125 |
| D | Massenet | Va! laisse couler mes larmes | Charlotte | *Werther* (III/fig 167) 2' | 126 |
| D | Menotti | Afraid, am I afraid? | Madame Flora/Baba | *The Medium* (II/fig 31–34) 2'45" | – |
| L | Meyerbeer | Nobles Seigneurs, salut! | Urbain | *Les Huguenots* (I/5B) 3'10" | 107 |
| A | Meyerbeer | Ah! mon fils sois béni | Fidès | *Le prophète* (II/10) 3'50" | 130 |
| L | Mozart | Parto, parto, ma tu ben mio | Sesto | *La clemenza di Tito* (I/9) 6'40" | 101 |
| L* | Mozart | Deh per questo istante solo | Sesto | *La clemenza di Tito* (II/19) 6'30" | 102 |
| L | Mozart | Smanie implacabili | Dorabella | *Così fan tutte* (I/11) 3'15" | 99 |
| L | Mozart | È amore un ladroncello | Dorabella | *Così fan tutte* (II/28) 3' | 100 |
| L | Mozart | Il padre adorato (Ah qual gelido orror) | Idamante | *Idomeneo* (I/7) 3'45" (+Recit) | – |

| Voice | Composer | Aria title | Character | Opera (Act/No.) | Aria No. |
|---|---|---|---|---|---|
| L | Mozart | Non so più cosa son, cosa faccio | Cherubino | Le nozze di Figaro (I/6) 2'40" | 97 |
| L | Mozart | Voi, che sapete che cosa è amor | Cherubino | Le nozze di Figaro (II/11) 2'30" | 98 |
| A | Musorgsky | Marfa's Prophecy (Sily potainye) | Marfa | Khovanschina (II/fig 182) 4'10" | EP47581 |
| A | Ponchielli | Voce di donna | La Cieca | La Gioconda (I) 2'45" | 134 |
| D | Ponchielli | Stella del marinar! | Laura | La Gioconda (II) 2'40" | – |
| A | Puccini | Se tu sapessi | Frugola | Il tabarro (fig 32) 2' | 135 |
| D | Purcell | Ah! Belinda | Dido | Dido and Aeneas (I) 3'45" | – |
| D | Purcell | Thy hand, Belinda | Dido | Dido and Aeneas (III) 3'45" | – |
| L | Rossini | Una voce poco fa | Rosina | Il barbiere di Siviglia (I/5) 5'30" (SI) | 104 |
| L* | Rossini | Nacqui all'affanno e al pianto (Non più mesta) | Cenerentola | La Cenerentola (II/Finale/fig 40) 6'20" | 105 |
| L | Rossini | Cruda sorte! | Isabella | L'italiana in Algeri (I/4) 4' | 103 |
| D | Rossini | Ah! quel giorno ognor rammento (Oh! Come da quel dì) | Arsace | Semiramide (I/2) 5'45" | – |
| D | Rossini | In sì barbara sciagura (Sì: vendicato) | Arsace | Semiramide (II/13) 3'15" + 3'30" (1v) | 115 |
| D | Rossini | Tu che accendi questo cor (Di tanti palpiti) | Tancredi | Tancredi (I/7) 3'30" | – |
| D | Saint-Saëns | Amour! Viens aider ma faiblesse! | Dalila | Samson et Dalila (II/sc 1) 4'40" | 123 |
| D | Saint-Saëns | Mon cœur s'ouvre à ta voix | Dalila | Samson et Dalila (II/sc 3) 5'40" | EP7553 |
| L | J. Strauss | Ich lade gern mit Gäste ein | Orlofsky | Die Fledermaus (II/7) 2'45" | 110 |
| D | R. Strauss | Sein wir wieder gut | Komponist | Ariadne auf Naxos (Prologue/fig 108) 2'45" | 128 |

| | | | | | |
|---|---|---|---|---|---|
| A | R. Strauss | Dein Zagen kenn ich | Gäa | *Daphne* (fig 58–67) 4'50" | — |
| D | R. Strauss | Ich habe keine guten Nächte | Klytämnestra | *Elektra* (fig 177–200) 5'45" | — |
| D | Stravinsky | Nonn'erubeskite, reges | Jocasta | *Oedipus Rex* (II/fig 94–117) 6'20" | — |
| D | Tchaikovsky | Da, chas nastal! | Joanna | *The Maid of Orleans* (I/7) 7' | 124 |
| L | Tchaikovsky | Ya nye spasobna k'grusti tomnoi | Olga | *Eugene Onegin* (I/3) 3'35" | 111 |
| A | Tchaikovsky | Padrugi miliye | Pauline | *Queen of Spades* (I/8) 2'30" | EP47581 |
| L | Thomas | Connais-tu le pays | Mignon | *Mignon* (I/4) 4'50" | 109 |
| L | Thomas | Styrienne (Je connais un pauvre enfant) | Mignon | *Mignon* (II/10) 3'15" | — |
| A | Verdi | Re dell'abisso, affrettati | Ulrica | *Un ballo in maschera* (I/2) 4'15" (SI) | 132 |
| D | Verdi | O don fatale | Eboli | *Don Carlo* (IV/sc 1) 5' | 119 |
| A | Verdi | Condotta ell'era in ceppi | Azucena | *Il trovatore* (II/10) 5'15" | 131 |
| A | Wagner | Weiche, Wotan | Erda | *Das Rheingold* (sc 4/fig 71) 4' | 133 |
| D | Wagner | Gerechter Gott (Wo war ich?) | Adriano | *Rienzi* (III/9) 6'50" + 2'45" | — |
| D | Wagner | So ist es denn aus | Fricka | *Die Walküre* (II/sc 1/fig 9A) 3'30" | 120 |
| D | Walton | I was a constant, faithful wife | Popova | *The Bear* (fig 69) 2'50" | — |
| L | Weber | Einst träumte meiner sel'gen Base | Ännchen | *Der Freischütz* (III/13) 5'40" | 106 |

# Tenor arias

**B** = Buffo  
**L** = Lyric  
**I** = Italian

**JH** = Youthful heroic  
**H** = Heroic

\* = Long aria (which may need to be cut)  
**SI** = Short introduction and/or playout  
Cabaletta or recitative title in brackets

| Voice | Composer | Aria title | Character | Opera (Act/No.) | Aria No. |
|---|---|---|---|---|---|
| JH | d'Albert | Traumerzählung (Wie ich nur gestern Abend) | Pedro | *Tiefland* (Vorspiel/sc 1) 3'15" | EP4233 |
| L | Barber | Outside this house | Anatol | *Vanessa* (II/fig 60) 3' | – |
| H | Beethoven | Gott! welch Dunkel hier! | Florestan | *Fidelio* (II/11) 6'10" (SI) | 189 |
| I | Bellini | Meco all'altar di Venere (Me protegge) | Pollione | *Norma* (I/sc 2) 3'15" + 2'45" | – |
| L | Berlioz | O blonde Cérès | Iopas | *Les troyens* (IV/sc 2/no 34) 3'50" | – |
| JH\* | Berlioz | Inutiles regrets | Énée | *Les troyens* (V/sc 1/no /41) 7'30" | EP7554 |
| JH | Bizet | La fleur que tu m'avais jetée | Don José | *Carmen* (II/17) 3'45" | 183 |
| L | Bizet | Je crois entendre encore (Recit. & Romance) | Nadir | *Les pêcheurs de perles* (I/4) 5' | EP7554 |

| | | | | | |
|---|---|---|---|---|---|
| L | Britten | Heaven helps those who help themselves | Albert | *Albert Herring* (II/sc 2/fig 85–95) 3'30" | 160 |
| L | Britten | It was out in the sticks | Inkslinger | *Paul Bunyan* (I/sc 2/no 14) 5'10" | – |
| JH | Britten | Go there! | Grimes | *Peter Grimes* (II/sc 2/fig 55–63) 5'45" | – |
| I | Cilea | L'anima ho stanca | Maurizio | *Adriana Lecouvreur* (II/fig 15) 1'25" | 175 |
| I | Cilea | Lamento di Federico (È la solita storia) | Federico | *L'arlesiana* (II/fig 15) 4' | 174 |
| L | Donizetti | Una furtiva lagrima | Nemorino | *L'elisir d'amore* (II/sc 8/fig 67) 3'45" | 147 |
| L | Donizetti | Spirito gentil | Fernando | *La favorita* (IV/fig 17) 2'30" | 149 |
| L | Donizetti | Pour mon âme | Tonio | *La fille du régiment* (I/fig 75) 4' | 148 |
| I | Donizetti | Fra poco a me ricovero (Tu che a Dio) | Edgardo | *Lucia di Lammermoor* (III/sc 2) 4'30" + 2'10" (SI) | 162 |
| L | Flotow | Ach! so fromm, ach so traut (M'appari) | Lionel | *Martha* (III/15) 2'50" | 150 |
| I | Giordano | Un dì all'azzurro spazio – Improvviso | Chénier | *Andrea Chénier* (I/fig 34) 4'30" | 172 |
| I | Giordano | Come un bel dì di maggio | Chénier | *Andrea Chénier* (IV/fig 1) 2'45" | 173 |
| I | Giordano | Amor ti vieta | Count Ipanov | *Fedora* (II) 1'35" | – |
| I | Gounod | Salut! demeure chaste et pure | Faust | *Faust* (III/8) 5'10" | 167 |
| L | Gounod | Ah, lève-toi, soleil! | Roméo | *Roméo et Juliette* (II/7) 4'15" | 154 |
| I | Halévy | Rachel, quand du seigneur (Va prononcer) | Éléazar | *La juive* (IV/22) 6'15" | EP7554 |
| L | Handel | Prigioniera ho l'alma in pena | Grimoaldo | *Rodelinda* (II/17) 6' | – |
| B | Lalo | Vainement, ma bien-aimée – Aubade | Mylio | *Le roi d'Ys* (III/fig 174) 3'15" | 138 |
| JH | Leoncavallo | Vesti la giubba | Canio | *I pagliacci* (I/end) 2'45" | 184 |
| B | Leoncavallo | O Colombina (Serenata) | Arlecchino/Beppe | *I pagliacci* (II) 2' | 139 |

| Voice | Composer | Aria title | Character | Opera (Act/No.) | Aria No. |
|---|---|---|---|---|---|
| JH | Mascagni | Siciliana | Turiddu | *Cavalleria rusticana* (Beginning) 1'55" | – |
| L | Massenet | En fermant les yeux (Le rêve) | Des Grieux | *Manon* (II/fig 133) 2'15" | 156 |
| L | Massenet | Ah! fuyez, douce image | Des Grieux | *Manon* (III/sc 2/fig 246) 4' | 157 |
| L | Massenet | Je ne sais si je veille | Werther | *Werther* (I/fig 21) 3'40" | EP7554 |
| L | Massenet | Pourquoi me réveiller | Werther | *Werther* (III/fig 190) 2'25" | 158 |
| L | Meyerbeer | Ô Paradis | Vasco de Gama | *L'africaine* (IV/15) 2'40" | 153 |
| JH | Mozart | Se all'impero, amici Dei! | Tito | *La clemenza di Tito* (II/20) 4'45" | 177 |
| L | Mozart | Un'aura amorosa | Ferrando | *Così fan tutte* (I/17) 3'30" | 143 |
| L | Mozart | Tradito, schernito dal perfido cor | Ferrando | *Così fan tutte* (II/27) 3' | – |
| L | Mozart | Hier soll ich dich denn sehen | Belmonte | *Die Entführung aus dem Serail* (I/1) 2'10" EP4233 | EP4233 |
| L | Mozart | O wie ängstlich | Belmonte | *Die Entführung aus dem Serail* (I/4) 5'20" | 140 |
| B | Mozart | Frisch zum Kampfe! | Pedrillo | *Die Entführung aus dem Serail* (II/13) 3'10" | 136 |
| L | Mozart | Wenn der Freude Thränen fliessen | Belmonte | *Die Entführung aus dem Serail* (II/15) 3'50" (short vers.) | EP736 /EP4233 |
| L* | Mozart | Ich baue ganz | Belmonte | *Die Entführung aus dem Serail* (III/17) 5'50" (SI) | – |
| L | Mozart | Dalla sua pace | Don Ottavio | *Don Giovanni* (I/11) 4'20" | 141 |
| L | Mozart | Il mio tesoro intanto | Don Ottavio | *Don Giovanni* (II/22) 4'15" | 142 |
| JH* | Mozart | Fuor del mar | Idomeneo | *Idomeneo* (II/12A unornamented) 5'15" | – |
| B | Mozart | In quegli anni, in cui val poco | Basilio | *Le nozze di Figaro* (IV/26) 3'30" EP8902/EP4233 | EP8902/EP4233 |

| | | | | | |
|---|---|---|---|---|---|
| L | Mozart | Dies Bildniss ist bezaubernd schön | Tamino | Die Zauberflöte (I/3) 3'35" | 144 |
| L | Nicolai | Horch, die Lerche singt im Hain | Fenton | Die lustigen Weiber von Windsor (II/7B) 4' | 151 |
| L | Offenbach | Legend of Kleinzach (Il était une fois) | Hoffmann | Les contes d'Hoffmann (Prologue/5) 3'40" | EP4233 |
| I | Ponchielli | Cielo! e mar! | Enzo | La Gioconda (II) 3'45" | 169 |
| I | Puccini | Che gelida manina | Rodolfo | La bohème (I/fig 30) 4'15" | 171 |
| I | Puccini | Addio fiorito asil | Pinkerton | Madama Butterfly (III/fig 27) 1'50" | – |
| JH | Puccini | Ch'ella mi creda | Johnson | La fanciulla del West (III/fig 26) 2'15" | 187 |
| L | Puccini | Firenze è come un albero fiorito | Rinuccio | Gianni Schicchi (fig 30) 2'20" | – |
| I | Puccini | Donna non vidi mai | Des Grieux | Manon Lescaut (I/fig 33) 2' | 170 |
| I | Puccini | Hal ben ragione | Luigi | Il tabarro (fig 44) 2'30" | 176 |
| JH | Puccini | Recondita armonia | Cavaradossi | Tosca (I/fig 17) 2'40" | 185 |
| JH | Puccini | E lucevan le stelle | Cavaradossi | Tosca (III/fig 11) 2'20" | 186 |
| JH | Puccini | Nessun dorma | Calaf | Turandot (III/sc I/fig 4) 2'35" | 188 |
| L | Rossini | Ecco ridente in cielo | Almaviva | Il barbiere di Siviglia (I/1) 3'20" (SI) | 146 |
| L | Rossini | Si, ritrovarla io giuro (Dolce speranza) | Don Ramiro | La Cenerentola (II) 3'20" + 1'45" (1v) | – |
| I | Rossini | Asile héréditaire | Arnold | Guillaume Tell (IV/19) 3'10" | EP7544 |
| L | Rossini | Languir per una bella (Contenta quest'alma) | Lindoro | L'italiana in Algeri (I/2) 2' (SI) + 3'35" | 145 |
| L | Smetana | Jak možná věřit | Jeník | The Bartered Bride (II/sc 5) 3'20" | – |
| B | Smetana | To, to me vhlavěleží | Vašek | The Bartered Bride (III/sc 1) 2'40" | 137 |
| L | Stravinsky | Here I stand | Tom Rakewell | The Rake's Progress (I/sc 1/fig 27) 2'45" | – |

| Voice | Composer | Aria title | Character | Opera (Act/No.) | Aria No. |
|---|---|---|---|---|---|
| L | Stravinsky | Love, too frequently betrayed | Tom Rakewell | The Rake's Progress (I/sc 2/fig 151) 2'45" | 161 |
| I | R. Strauss | Di rigori amato il seno | Italian Singer | Der Rosenkavalier (I/fig 233) 2' | – |
| L | Tchaikovsky | Kuda, kuda | Lenski | Eugene Onegin (II/17 sc 2) 5'30" | 155 |
| L | Thomas | Adieu, Mignon, courage! | Wilhelm | Mignon (II/11) 3'40" | – |
| L | Thomas | Elle ne croyait pas | Wilhelm | Mignon (III/14) 3'10" | EP7554 |
| JH | Verdi | Celeste Aida | Radames | Aida (I) 4'15" | 182 |
| JH | Verdi | Ma se m'è forza perderti (Forse la soglia) | Riccardo | Un ballo in maschera (III/sc 2/fig 36) | – |
| JH | Verdi | Io là vidi | Carlo | Don Carlo (Fontainebleau scene) 3'30" | EP4248 |
| L | Verdi | Dal labbro il canto | Fenton | Falstaff (III/sc 2/fig 23) 2'15" (SI) | 159 |
| JH | Verdi | Oh, tu che in seno angl' angeli (Della natal) | Alvaro | La forza del destino (III/16) 3'45" | 181 |
| I | Verdi | Quando le sere al placido | Rodolfo | Luisa Miller (II finale/fig 37) | 163 |
| I | Verdi | Ah, la paterna mano (O figli) | Macduff | Macbeth (IV/sc 1/no 18) 3'30" | 168 |
| H | Verdi | Dio! mi potevi scagliar tutti i mali | Otello | Otello (III/sc 3/letter N) 3'30" | 191 |
| I | Verdi | Questa o quella | Il Duca | Rigoletto (I) 2' | 164 |
| I | Verdi | Parmi veder le lagrime | Il Duca | Rigoletto (II) 5' | 165 |
| I | Verdi | La donna è mobile | Il Duca | Rigoletto (III) 2'10" | 166 |
| L | Verdi | De' miei bollenti spiriti | Alfredo | La traviata (II) 3'5" | 152 |
| L | Verdi | Ah sì, ben mio | Manrico | Il trovatore (III/18/sc 2) 2'45" | – |
| JH* | Verdi | Di quella pira | Manrico | Il trovatore (III/18/sc 2) 2'15" (1v) | EP4248 |
| JH | Wagner | Willst jenes Tag's du nicht dich mehr entsinnen | Erik | Der fliegende Holländer (III/8A or 9A) 2'45" | 179 |

| | | | | | |
|---|---|---|---|---|---|
| JH | Wagner | In fernem Land | Lohengrin | *Lohengrin* (III/sc 2/fig 61) 4' | EP736 |
| JH | Wagner | Mein lieber Schwan! | Lohengrin | *Lohengrin* (III/sc 2/fig 74) 4'20" | 180 |
| JH | Wagner | Morgenlich leuchtend – Prize Song | Walther | *Die Meistersinger von Nürnberg* (III/sc 2/fig 198 – 202) 4'15" (3vv) | EP736 |
| H | Wagner | Notung! Notung! – Forging Song | Siegfried | *Siegfried* (I/sc 3/fig 110A) 3' | – |
| JH* | Wagner | Inbrunst im Herzen – Romerzählung | Tannhäuser | *Tannhäuser* (III/sc 3/fig 141–147) 11'10" | – |
| H | Wagner | Ein Schwert verhiess mir der Vater | Siegmund | *Die Walküre* (I/sc 3/fig 40) | – |
| H | Wagner | Winterstürme | Siegmund | *Die Walküre* (I/sc 3/fig 558) 3'30" | 190 |
| JH* | Weber | Durch die Wälder | Max | *Der Freischütz* (I/3) 6'45" | 178 |
| L | Weill | At night when everything – Lonely House | Sam | *Street Scene* (I/10) 2'50" | – |

# Baritone arias

L = Lyric
C = Character
K = Cavalier

H = Heroic
* = Long aria (which may need to be cut)
SI = Short introduction and/or playout

Cabaletta or recitative title in brackets

| Voice | Composer | Aria title | Character | Opera (Act/No.) | Aria No. |
|---|---|---|---|---|---|
| H | Beethoven | Ha! welch' ein Augenblick! | Pizarro | *Fidelio* (I/7) 3'20" | EP4234 |
| K | Bellini | Ah! per sempre io ti perdei (Or dove) | Riccardo | *I puritani* (I/2) 4'10" | 200 |
| C | Berlioz | Chanson de la puce (Une puce gentille) | Méphistophélès | *La damnation de Faust* (II/sc 6) 1'30" | – |
| C | Bizet | Votre toast, je peux vous le rendre | Escamillo | *Carmen* (II/13 or 14) 4' | 213 |
| K | Bizet | O Nadir, tendre ami (L'orage s'est calmé) | Zurga | *Les pêcheurs de perles* (III/11) 5'15" (SI) | 204 |
| H | Borodin | Ni sna, ni otdikha izmuchennoi dushe | Prince Igor | *Prince Igor* (II/13) 5'15" | 223 |
| K | Britten | Look! Through the port comes the moonshine astray! | Billy Budd | *Billy Budd* (IV/sc 1) 5'10" | 207 |
| L | Donizetti | Come Paride vezzoso | Belcore | *L'elisir d'amore* (I/fig 29) 2'55" | 195 |
| K | Donizetti | Cruda, funesta smania (La pietade) | Enrico | *Lucia di Lammermoor* (I/sc 1) 1'50" + 1'30" (1v) | 199 |

| | | | | | |
|---|---|---|---|---|---|
| L | Donizetti | Bella siccome un angelo | Malatesta | Don Pasquale (I/sc 1) 2'40" | 196 |
| C | Giordano | Nemico della Patria?! | Gérard | Andrea Chénier (III/fig 12) 4'15" | 219 |
| K | Gounod | Avant de quitter ces lieux | Valentine | Faust (II/4) 3'40" | 203 |
| L | Gounod | Ballade de la reine Mab | Mercutio | Roméo et Juliette (I/2) 2'40" | — |
| L | Korngold | Mein Sehnen, Mein Wähnen – Pierrot's Lied | Fritz | Die tote Stadt (fig 169) 3'25" | — |
| L | Lehár | O Vaterland du machst bei Tag | Danilo | Die lustige Witwe (I/4) 2'40" | — |
| C | Leoncavallo | Si può? | Tonio | I pagliacci (Prologue) 4'15" | 217 |
| C | Massenet | Vision fugitive | Hérode | Hérodiade (II/sc 5) 2'50" | 215 |
| K | Meyerbeer | Ah mon remords te venge | Hoël | Dinorah (III/25) 3' | — |
| L | Mozart | Rivolgete a lui lo sguardo | Guglielmo | Così fan tutte (I/15A) 5'30" | — |
| L | Mozart | Donne mie, la fate a tanti | Guglielmo | Così fan tutte (II/26) 3'10" | 192 |
| K | Mozart | Fin ch'han dal vino | Don Giovanni | Don Giovanni (I/12) 1'35" | EP737/EP4234 |
| K | Mozart | Deh, vieni alla finestra | Don Giovanni | Don Giovanni (II/17) 2'10" | EP737/EP4234 |
| K | Mozart | Vedrò, mentr'io sospiro (Hai già vinta la causa) | Il Conte | Le nozze di Figaro (III/17) 4'30" | 198 |
| L | Mozart | Der Vogelfänger bin ich ja | Papageno | Die Zauberflöte (I/2) 2'40" (3vv) | EP737/EP4234 |
| L | Mozart | Ein Mädchen oder Weibchen | Papageno | Die Zauberflöte (II/20) 3' (2vv) | 193 |
| C | Offenbach | Scintille diamant | Dapertutto | Les contes d'Hoffmann (II/15) 2' | 214 |
| L | Ponchielli | Ah! pescator, affonda l'esca | Barnaba | La Gioconda (II) 2'15" | 197 |

| Voice | Composer | Aria title | Character | Opera (Act/No.) | Aria No. |
|---|---|---|---|---|---|
| K | Puccini | Questo amor, vergogna mia | Frank | *Edgar* (I/fig 21) 2'30" | 206 |
| C | Puccini | Ah che zucconi! | Gianni Schicci | *Gianni Schicci* (fig 49) 2'10" | – |
| C | Puccini | Nulla! Silenzio! | Michele | *Il tabarro* (fig 86) 3' | 220 |
| C | Rachmaninov | Ves tabor spit | Alekho | *Alekho* (no 10) 5'15" (SI) | EP7583 |
| L | Rossini | Largo al factotum | Figaro | *Il barbiere di Siviglia* (I/2) 5' | 194 |
| L | Rossini | Come un'ape ne' giorni d'aprile | Dandini | *La Cenerentola* (I) 5'15" (1v) | – |
| H | Rossini | Sois immobile | Tell | *Guillaume Tell* (III/sc 3/no 18) 2'30" | – |
| K | Tchaikovsky | Vï mne pisali | Onegin | *Eugene Onegin* (I/12 sc 3) 5'10" | 205 |
| K | Tchaikovsky | Ya vas lyublyu (Vï tak pichalni) | Yeletsky | *Queen of Spades* (II/12) 4'15" | EP7583 |
| C | Thomas | O vin, dissipe la tristesse | Hamlet | *Hamlet* (II/10) 3'15" | – |
| C | Verdi | Eri tu | Renato | *Un ballo in maschera* (III/fig 7) 5' | 210 |
| C | Verdi | Per me giunto è il dì supremo (O Carlo, ascolta) | Rodrigo | *Don Carlo* (IV/sc 2) 3'30" + 3'20" | 212 |
| C | Verdi | È sogno? o realtà | Ford | *Falstaff* (II/sc 1 /fig 19) 4'30" | 218 |
| C | Verdi | Urna fatale | Don Carlo | *La forza del destino* (III/20/sc 2) 4'40" | 211 |
| H | Verdi | Pietà, rispetto, amore | Macbeth | *Macbeth* (IV/sc 3/no 20) 4'15" | 221 |
| C | Verdi | Credo in un Dio crudel | Iago | *Otello* (II/sc 2/letter C) 4'45" | 216 |
| C | Verdi | Cortigiani, vil razza | Rigoletto | *Rigoletto* (II) 3'50" | 208 |
| K | Verdi | Di Provenza il mar | Germont | *La traviata* (II/10) 4'5" | 202 |
| C | Verdi | Il balen del suo sorriso | Conte di Luna | *Il trovatore* (II/12/sc 2) 4'45" | 209 |

| | | | | | |
|---|---|---|---|---|---|
| H* | Wagner | Wahn! Wahn! | Sachs | *Die Meistersinger von Nürnburg* (III/sc 1/fig {120) 6'20" | EP737 |
| H* | Wagner | Wehvolles Erbe | Amfortas | *Parsifal* (II/sc 2/fig 105) 8' | – |
| H | Wagner | Mein Vater! | Amfortas | *Parsifal* (III/sc 2/fig 277) 4'30" | 222 |
| K | Wagner | O du mein holder Abendstern | Wolfram | *Tannhäuser* (III/sc 2/fig 135) 4'30" | 201 |
| H* | Wagner | Leb' wohl, du kühnes, herrliches Kind! | Wotan | *Die Walküre* (III/sc 3/fig 84) 10' | – |

# Bass arias

**B** = Buffo

**BB** = Bass-baritone

**S** = Basso-profondo (Seriöso)

\* = Long aris (which may need to be cut)

**SI** = Short introduction and/or playout

Cabaletta or recitative title in brackets

| Voice | Composer | Aria title | Character | Opera (Act/No.) | Aria No. |
|---|---|---|---|---|---|
| BB | Beethoven | Hat man nicht auch Gold beineben | Rocco | Fidelio (I/4) 2'40" | EP4235/EP737 |
| S | Bellini | Vi ravviso, o luoghi ameni (Tu non sai) | Conte Rodolfo | La sonnambula (I/6) 2'15" + 2'20" (1v) | 236 |
| S | Borodin | O niet, niet, drug | Khan Kontchak | Prince Igor (II) 4'30" | – |
| BB | Britten | O beauty, O handsomeness, goodnessN | Claggart | Billy Budd (I/sc 3/fig 105) 5'15" | 233 |
| B | Britten | When my cue comes – Bottom's Dream | Bottom | A Midsummer Night's Dream (III/fig 25) 4'10" | 227 |
| B | Donizetti | Ah! un foco insolito | Pasquale | Don Pasquale (I/sc 1) 2'20" | – |
| BB | Gounod | Le veau d'or est toujours debout! | Méphistophélès | Faust (II/4) 2'10" | 232 |
| BB | Gounod | Sérénade | Méphistophélès | Faust (IV/15) 2'30" | – |
| S | Halévy | Si la rigueur et la vengeance | Brogni | La juive (I/2) 3'20" | – |
| BB | Handel | Sorge infausta (O voi, del mio poter) | Zoaster | Orlando (III/sc 6) 5'30" | – |

| | | | | | |
|---|---|---|---|---|---|
| S | Massenet | Épouse quelque brave fille (Les grands mots) | Comte des Grieux | *Manon* (III/sc 2/fig 240) 2'15" | — |
| B* | Mozart | Solche hergelauf'ne Laffen | Osmin | *Die Entführung aus dem Serail* (I/3) 4'15" (SI) | 224 |
| B | Mozart | Ha! wie will ich triumphieren | Osmin | *Die Entführung aus dem Serail* (III/19) 3'55" | — |
| B | Mozart | Madamina! (Eh consolatevi) | Leporello | *Don Giovanni* (I/4) 5'50" | 226 |
| BB | Mozart | Se vuol ballare (Bravo, Signor padrone) | Figaro | *Le nozze di Figaro* (I/3) 3'5" | 228 |
| B | Mozart | La vendetta (Bene, io tutto farò) | Bartolo | *Le nozze di Figaro* (I/4) 3' | 225 |
| BB | Mozart | Non più andrai | Figaro | *Le nozze di Figaro* (I/9) 3'20" (SI) | 229 |
| BB | Mozart | Aprite un po' quegl'occhi | Figaro | *Le nozze di Figaro* (IV/26) 3'45" | 230 |
| S | Mozart | O Isis und Osiris | Sarastro | *Die Zauberflöte* (II/10) 2'30" | 234 |
| S | Mozart | In diesen heil'gen Hallen | Sarastro | *Die Zauberflöte* (II/15) 3'30" | 235 |
| BB | Musorgsky | Dostig ya vishei vlasti – Monologue | Boris | *Boris Godunov* (II/fig 43) 5'15" | — |
| S | Puccini | Vecchia zimarra | Colline | *La bohème* (IV/fig 19) 1'50" | 243 |
| BB* | Rossini | La calunnia | Basilio | *Il barbiere di Siviglia* (I/6) 3'45" (with cut) | 231 |
| B* | Rossini | A un dottor | Bartolo | *Il barbiere di Siviglia* (I/8) 6'35" | EP4235 |
| B | Rossini | Già d'insolito ardore | Mustapha | *L'italiana in Algeri* (I/6) 4' | — |
| BB | Rossini | Là nel ciel nell'arcano profondo | Alidoro | *La cenerentola* (I/Appendix) 2'40" | — |
| S | Tchaikovsky | Lyubvi vse vozrasti pakorni | Gremin | *Eugene Onegin* (III/20A/sc 1) 5'30" | 242 |
| S | Tchaikovsky | Gospod moi, yesli greshen, ya | King René | *Yolanta* (fig 110) 3'45" | — |
| S | Verdi | Ella giammai m'amò | Filippo | *Don Carlo* (IV/sc 1) 6' (SI) | 241 |

| Voice | Composer | Aria title | Character | Opera (Act/No.) | Aria No. |
|---|---|---|---|---|---|
| S | Verdi | Infelice! ... e tuo credevi | Silva | *Ernani* (I/Finale) 2'30" | 237 |
| S | Verdi | Come dal ciel precipita (Studia il passo) | Banco | *Macbeth* (II/sc 2/no 10) 4' | 240 |
| S | Verdi | Il lacerato spirito | Fiesco | *Simon Boccanegra* (Prologue/letter P) 3'20" | 239 |
| S | Verdi | O tu, Palermo | Procida | *I vespri Siciliani* (II/7) 4' | 238 |
| S | Wagner | Hier sitz'ich zur Wacht | Hagen | *Götterdämmerung* (I/sc 2/fig 60) 4'30" | – |
| BB | Wagner | Mögst du mein Kind, den fremden Mann willkommen heissen | Daland | *Der fliegende Holländer* (II/6) 4'30" | – |
| BB | Weill | Let things be like they always was | Maurrant | *Street Scene* (I/8) 3'20" | – |

# French Operatic Arias

As EVERY SINGER and lover of French opera knows, editions of even the best-known French operatic arias are difficult – and sometimes expensive – to obtain. Roger Nichols' scrupulously balanced selection of 19th-century French arias provides the perfect starting point for wider exploration. Nichols, who has championed French music in his writings, talks and radio broadcasts over three decades with eloquence and scholarship, is the ideal guide to this repertoire which, even today, is often neglected, misunderstood or inadequately performed.

– Sir John Elliot Gardiner

| French Operatic Arias for Soprano | EP 7552 | £14.95 |
| French Operatic Arias for Mezzo-Soprano | EP 7553 | £14.95 |
| French Operatic Arias for Tenor | EP 7554 | £14.95 |
| French Operatic Arias for Baritone | EP 7555 | £14.95 |
| French Operatic Arias for Bass | EP 7556 | £14.95 |

# Opera aria albums

Published by Peters Edition

## Soprano

**Aria Album** (Dörffel / Soldan)
Soprano: 58 Arias (Ger./It./Fr.)
£19.50  EP 734

**Bel Canto Album** (It.) (Landshoff)
Vol.1: 29 Arias
£13.95  EP 3348a
Vol.2: 21 Arias
£13.95  EP 3348c

**Coloratura Album**
(Ger., with some It./Fr.)
24 Soprano Arias
£19.50  EP 2074

**French Operatic Arias** (Fr.) (Nichols)
£14.95  EP 7552

**Opera Arias** (Ger., with some also It./Fr.)
Soprano Vol.1: 36 Arias
£17.90  EP 4231a
Soprano Vol.2: 44 Arias
£17.90  EP 4231b

**Russian Operatic Arias** (Fanning)
*in preparation*  EP 7580

**Soprano Arias**
£23.00  EP 9995a

**9 Selected Opera Arias**
£5.50  EP 10846

## Mezzo-Soprano

**Aria Album** (Dörffel / Soldan)
Mezzo-Soprano: 19 Arias (Ger./It.)
£11.95  EP 794

**French Operatic Arias** (Fr.) (Nichols)
£14.95  EP 7553

**Opera Arias** (Ger., with some also It./Fr.)
Contralto (Mezzo-Soprano): 34 Arias
£15.95  EP 4232

**Russian Operatic Arias** (Fanning)
*in preparation*  EP 7581

## Contralto

**Aria Album** (Dörffel / Soldan)
Contralto: 55 Arias (Ger./Eng./It./Lat.)
£18.95  EP 735

**Opera Arias** (Ger., with some also It./Fr.)
Contralto (Mezzo-Soprano): 34 Arias
**£15.95** EP 4232

# Tenor

**Aria Album** (Dörffel / Soldan)
Tenor: 40 Arias (Ger./It./Fr.)
**£15.95** EP 736

**French Operatic Arias** (Fr.) (Nichols)
**£14.95** EP 7554

**Opera Arias** (Ger., with some also It./Fr.)
Tenor: 47 Arias
**£18.95** EP 4233

**Russian Operatic Arias** (Fanning)
*in preparation* EP 7582

# Baritone

**Aria Album** (Dörffel / Soldan)
Baritone & Bass: 54 Arias
(Ger./It./Fr./Eng.)
**£19.50** EP 737

**French Operatic Arias** (Fr.) (Nichols)
**£14.95** EP 7555

**Opera Arias** (Ger., with some also It./Fr.)
Baritone: 30 Arias.
**£15.95** EP 4234

**Russian Operatic Arias** (Fanning)
in preparation EP 7583

# Bass

**Bass Album** (Ger.)
25 Lieder and Arias from Handel to Wolf
**£9.50** EP 2817

**French Operatic Arias** (Fr.) (Nichols)
**£14.95** EP 7556

**Opera Arias** (Ger., with some also It./Fr.)
Bass: 36 Arias
**£17.90** EP 4235

**Russian Operatic Arias** (Fanning)
*in preparation* EP 7584

# Opera vocal scores

Published by Peters Edition

## Beethoven, L. van
**Fidelio** (Ger.)
£15.95  EP 44

## Bizet, G.
**Carmen** (Fr./Eng.) (Langham Smith)
*in preparation*  EP 7548

**Carmen** (Ger.)
£19.50  EP 3001

## Borodin, A.P.
**Prince Igor**  (Russ./Fr./Ger.)
Cloth bound
£48.00  BEL 477+

## Donizetti, G.
**La fille du regiment**
£29.00  EP 1813a

## Dove, J.
**Flight**
£29.95  EP 7511

**Tobias and the Angel**
£24.95  EP 7535
Church Opera in one act

## Flotow, F.
**Martha** (Ger.)
£23.00  EP 3480

## Gluck, C.W.
**Orpheus** (Fr./Ger.)
£15.95  EP 54a

## Gounod, C.
**Faust** (Fr./Ger.)
£23.00  EP 4402

## Handel, G.F.

**Julius Caesar** (Ger./It.)
£17.90   EP 3783

**Rodelinde** (Ger./It.)
£15.95   EP 3784

**Xerxes** (Ger.)
£15.95   EP 3792

## Humperdinck, E.

**Hänsel und Gretel** (Ger.)
£15.50   EP 9249

## Lortzing, A.

**Zar und Zimmerman** (Ger.)
£23.00   EP 2051

**Undine** (Ger.)
£23.00   EP 2053

**Der Waffenschmied** (Ger.)
£23.00   EP 2052

**Der Wildschütz** (Ger.)
£23.00   EP 2054

## Mascagni, P.

**Cavalleria rusticana** (Ger./It.)
£19.50   EP 4400

## Mendelssohn, F.

**A Midsummer Night's Dream** (Ger.)
£8.25   EP 1751

## Mozart, W.A.

**Bastien und Bastienne** (Ger.)
£11.95   EP 9001

**Così fan tutte** (Ger./It.)
£23.00   EP 4474

**La clemenza di Tito** (Ger./It.)
£15.95   EP 746

**Don Giovanni** (Ger./It.)
£19.50   EP 4473

**Die Entführung aus dem Serail /
Il seraglio** (Ger.)
£16.50   EP 745

**Idomeneo** (Ger./It.)
£25.00   EP 1127

**Impresario** (Ger.)
£6.95   EP 2184

**The Magic Flute / Die Zauberflöte** (Ger.)
£11.95   EP 71

**The Marriage of Figaro** (Ger./It.)
£19.50   EP 4472

## Nicolai, O.

**The Merry Wives of Windsor** (Ger.)
£26.00   EP 1940

## Offenbach, J.

**Tales of Hoffmann** (Ger.)
£26.00   EP 3269

## Puccini, G.

**Madam Butterfly** (It./Ger.)
£23.00   EP 9635

## Rimsky-Korsakov, N.

**The Golden Cockerel** (Ger./Eng.)
£23.00   EP 8006

## Rossini, G.

**The Barber of Seville** (Ger./It.)
£29.00   EP 4265

## Smetana, B.

**The Bartered Bride** (Ger.)
£23.00   EP 4403

## Strauss, J.

**Die Fledermaus** (Ger.) (Freyer)
£23.00   EP 9777

## Verdi, G.

**Aida** (Ger./It.)
£19.50  EP 4253

**Don Carlos** (Ger.)
£18.95  EP 4534

**La forza del destino** (Ger./It.)
£18.95  EP 4254

**Rigoletto** (Ger./It.)
£18.95  EP 2185

**La traviata** (Ger./It.)
£18.95  EP 1469

**Il trovatore** (Ger./It.)
£18.95  EP 1379

## Wagner, R.

**The Flying Dutchman** (Ger.)
£19.50  EP 3402

**Lohengrin** (Ger.)
£19.50  EP 3401

**The Mastersingers
of Nuremberg** (Ger.)
£26.00  EP 3408

**Parsifal** (Ger.)
£19.50  EP 3409

**Tannhäuser** (Ger.)
£33.00  EP 8217

**Tristan and Isolde** (Ger.)
£21.00  EP 3407

**The Ring of the Nibelung
  Das Rheingold** (Ger.)
  £19.50  EP 3403

  **Die Walküre** (Ger.)
  £19.50  EP 3404

  **Siegfried** (Ger.)
  £19.50  EP 3405

  **Götterdämmerung** (Ger.)
  £19.50  EP 3406

## Weber, C.M. von

**Abu Hassan** (Ger.)
£25.00  EP 9743

**Der Freischütz** (Ger.)
£15.95  EP 9741

**Oberon** (Ger.)
£18.95  EP 3010a

**Peter Schmoll** (Ger.)
£18.95  EP 4834

## Wolf, H.

**Der Corregidor** (Ger.)
£23.00  EP 3730

Please Note
Prices are correct at time of going to
press, but must be subject to change
without notice

# Composer opera aria albums

Published by Peters Edition

## Mozart, W.A.
**Famous Opera Arias** (It./Ger.)
Soprano
£5.50  EP 8901

Tenor
£5.50  EP 8902

Bass
£5.50  EP 8903

## Verdi, G.
**30 Soprano Arias** (It./Ger.) (Soldan)
Vol.1
£13.95  EP 4246a
Vol.2
£13.95  EP 4246b

**7 Mezzo-Soprano Arias** (It./Ger.) (Soldan)
£9.50  EP 4247

**23 Tenor Arias** (It./Ger.) (Soldan)
£13.95  EP 4248

**20 Baritone Arias** (It./Ger.) (Soldan)
£13.95  EP 4249

**13 Bass Arias** (It./Ger.) (Soldan)
£13.95  EP 4245

## The Peters Vocal Guide
(EP 7603) includes contents listings
for all vocal albums published by
Peters Edition.

Copies are available from all
good music shops or from:
ⓒ marketing@uk.edition-peters.com
ⓣ 020 7553 4000

*Please Note*
Prices are correct at time of going to
press, but must be subject to change
without notice